Treaty Talks in British Columbia

Christopher McKee

Treaty Talks in British Columbia:
Negotiating a Mutually
Beneficial Future

UBCPress/Vancouver

© UBC Press 1996

Printed in Canada on acid-free paper ∞
ISBN 0-7748-0586-2 (hardcover)
ISBN 0-7748-0587-0 (paperback)

Canadian Cataloguing in Publication Data
McKee, Christopher, 1964–
  Treaty talks in British Columbia

  Includes bibliographic references and index.
  ISBN 0-7748-0586-2 (bound)
  ISBN 0-7748-0587-0 (pbk.)

  1. Indians of North America – British Columbia – Claims. 2. Indians of North America – British Columbia – Land tenure. 3. Indians of North America – Canada – Government relations. 4. Indians of North America – British Columbia – Claims – History. 5. Indians of North America – British Columbia – Land tenure – History. I. Title.

KEB529.4.M43 1996   333.2   C96-910499-5
KF8208.M34 1996

This book has been published with the help of a grant from the British Columbia Treaty Commission.

UBC Press gratefully acknowledges the ongoing support to its publishing program from the Canada Council, the Province of British Columbia Cultural Services Branch, and the Department of Communications of the Government of Canada.

UBC Press
University of British Columbia
6344 Memorial Road
Vancouver, BC V6T 1Z2
(604) 822-3259
Fax: 1-800-668-0821
E-mail: orders@ubcpress.ubc.ca
http://www.ubcpress.ubc.ca

This book is dedicated to Bernadee and Margaret.
They have given me their unqualified support for everything I
have done, and have enabled me to see through the guise of
everyday events.

Contents

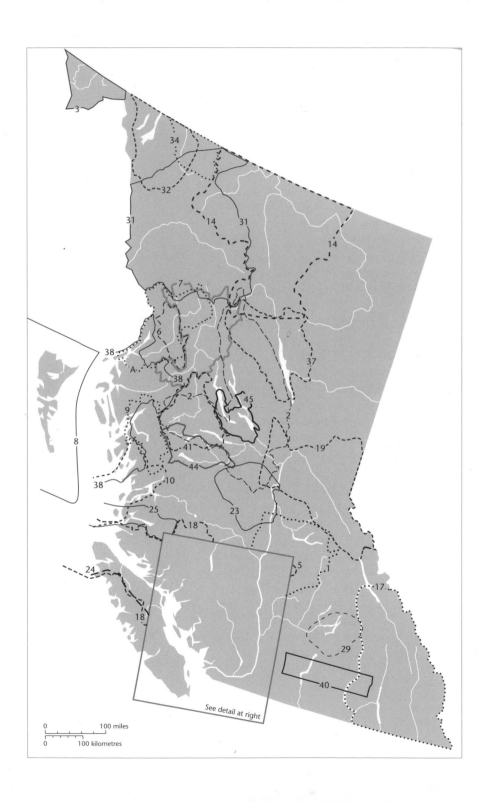

See detail at right

0   100 miles

0   100 kilometres

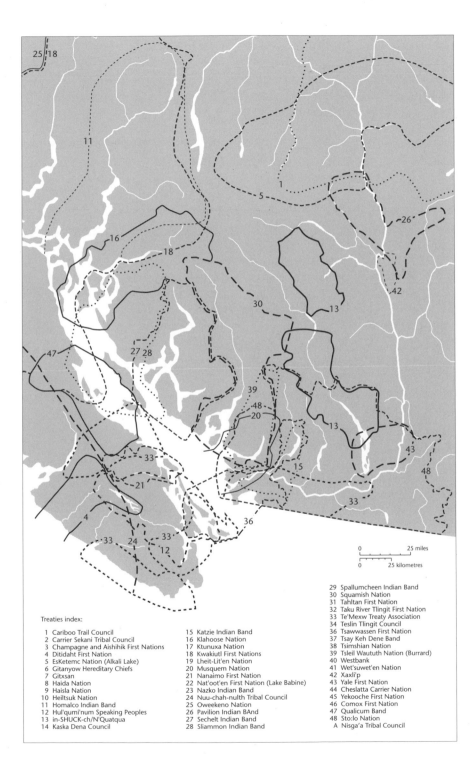

Treaties index:

1 Cariboo Trail Council
2 Carrier Sekani Tribal Council
3 Champagne and Aishihik First Nations
4 Ditidaht First Nation
5 EsKetemc Nation (Alkali Lake)
6 Gitanyow Hereditary Chiefs
7 Gitxsan
8 Haida Nation
9 Haisla Nation
10 Heiltsuk Nation
11 Homalco Indian Band
12 Hul'qumi'num Speaking Peoples
13 in-SHUCK-ch/N'Quatqua
14 Kaska Dena Council

15 Katzie Indian Band
16 Klahoose Nation
17 Ktunuxa Nation
18 Kwakiutl First Nations
19 Lheit-Lit'en Nation
20 Musquem Nation
21 Nanaimo First Nation
22 Nat'oot'en First Nation (Lake Babine)
23 Nazko Indian Band
24 Nuu-chah-nulth Tribal Council
25 Oweekeno Nation
26 Pavilion Indian BAnd
27 Sechelt Indian Band
28 Sliammon Indian Band

29 Spallumcheen Indian Band
30 Squamish Nation
31 Tahltan First Nation
32 Taku River Tlingit First Nation
33 Te'Mexw Treaty Association
34 Teslin Tlingit Council
36 Tsawwassen First Nation
37 Tsay Keh Dene Band
38 Tsimshian Nation
39 Tsleil Waututh Nation (Burrard)
40 Westbank
41 Wet'suwet'en Nation
42 Xaxli'p
43 Yale First Nation
44 Cheslatta Carrier Nation
45 Yekooche First Nation
46 Comox Nation
47 Qualicum Band
48 Sto:lo Nation
 A Nisga'a Tribal Council

Acknowledgments

I would like to express my sincere gratitude to the several individuals who assisted me in the production of this book. Professor Paul Tennant of the Department of Political Science at the University of British Columbia gave me some initial ideas for the book and offered some very helpful comments after reading an earlier draft. Dr Paul Kariya and Peter Colenbrander of the British Columbia Treaty Commission offered assistance in many ways, and Dr Peter Lusztig, also of the commission, suggested the inclusion of some additional material. Chief Gary Feschuk and Tom Paul provided information on and insight into the Sechelt treaty negotiations. Chuck Connaghan, former chief commissioner of the British Columbia Treaty Commission, offered comments after reading an earlier version of the book. Jack Hughes of Indian and Northern Affairs Canada provided assistance in clarifying some legal issues.

Chief Don Ryan of the Gitxsan provided commentary and more than frank answers to my questions, and Chief Elmer Derrick offered additional ideas on changes to the treaty-making process. Nelson Keitlah of the Nuu'Chah'Nulth Tribal Council gave information on their negotiations. Murray Rankin and Dan Johnston of the Ministry of Aboriginal Affairs in Victoria also gave assistance. Several members of the Treaty Negotiation Advisory Committee provided me with valuable information and interviews. They include: Mike Hunter of the Fisheries Council of British Columbia; Marlie Beets of the Council of Forest Industries; Bill Wimpney of the British Columbia Wildlife Federation; Guy Rose of the Cattlemen's Association of British Columbia; and Ted George of the British Columbia Chamber of Commerce. I would also like to thank the federal and provincial officials I interviewed, for their insight and information.

A final note of thanks is extended to the British Columbia Treaty Commission for providing the funds necessary to complete this book. The commission saw the need to raise the level of public awareness surrounding treaty negotiations through the production of an informed, written account. They maintained an arms-length approach to this project from the outset, leaving me free to explore and to write about those issues I felt deserved attention.

Introduction

The treaty-making process in British Columbia is a controversial but little understood issue in the province. Since 1993 the issue has become polarized, with opponents characterizing the negotiations as secretive, exclusive of non-aboriginal interests, and on the verge of a massive give-away of British Columbia's land and natural resources to aboriginal groups. Proponents of the process argue that it is a long overdue recognition of aboriginal title and other aboriginal rights, and a means whereby First Nations can secure a measure of self-sufficiency and a return to their original status as complex and self-governing entities.

These divergent views have created the need for a perspective on the treaty-making process that occupies a middle ground and that does not accept the arguments of either the opponents or proponents of Native land claims unequivocally. This book attempts to offer such a perspective, providing the lay reader with an informed account of the treaty-making process during its first two years of operation. It aims to provide some answers to questions surrounding the debate that have not been dealt with elsewhere in a succinct fashion, nor placed within their historical, legal, and political context. Some of the general questions this book examines are:

- Why is the British Columbia government negotiating treaties with aboriginal groups in the province?
- How is a treaty concluded?
- Who is participating in the negotiation of treaties?
- Who pays for the treaty negotiations?
- What are some of the costs of negotiating treaties?
- What are some of the problems of the treaty-making process to date?
- What consequences will there be as a result of negotiating treaties?

Earlier works have provided a solid foundation for a book of this sort. Robin Fisher's *Contact and Conflict*[1] sought to address the limited view provided by historians up to that point of indigenous peoples in Canada. His book deals with the history of contact between Indian and European cultures in a general way, and examines, specifically, Indian-European relations in British Columbia from 1774 to 1890. Frank Cassidy and Norman Dale provided a look into the future in *After Native Claims?*[2] by painting a literary picture of what might happen to natural resource use and management in British Columbia as a result of comprehensive claim settlements, which, at the time of publication in 1988, had reached an impasse. The concern of these authors centred on how resolving issues related to comprehensive claims might affect the economic, political, and environmental dimensions of natural resource activities. Their additional concern was to address and clarify the issues underlying Native land claims in order to add a measure of certainty about what was (and to a large extent continues to be) at stake, and to provide greater insight into how Native claims might be resolved.

Paul Tennant's *Aboriginal Peoples and Politics*[3] did a great service, especially to those concerned with the political dimension of the question. Indeed, it provided the first comprehensive account of the Indian land question in the province and was the first to examine the modern political history of British Columbia's aboriginal people. Unfortunately, Tennant's book concluded just as the provincial government had reversed its long-standing policy of denying aboriginal title and refusing to negotiate with aboriginal groups. And Mel Smith's *Our Home or Native Land?*[4] – the most recent contribution to the debate – sought to offer a polemic on Canada's aboriginal policy. Due largely to the time at which the book was written, Smith's treatment of the treaty-making process was scant, and left many questions unanswered.

Chapter 1 of this book deals with British Columbia's aboriginal people, the history of aboriginal-government relations, and legal concepts relating to Native people. The first section offers the reader a brief survey of the sociopolitical organization of Native people in the province, prior to and after European contact. The second section provides brief summaries of major aspects of the law relating to Native people. It discusses aboriginal rights, and addresses both the source of such rights and the bases on which an aboriginal right can be extinguished. The section also discusses aboriginal treaties, the notion of aboriginal title, and the concept of aboriginal self-government. The third section deals with the major events in the province that led to the initiation of the current treaty-making process. The early treaty-making process in the colony is discussed, with particular reference to the Douglas purchase treaties on Vancouver Island

and the Treaty Eight adhesions in the Peace River district. The section also looks at the efforts of colonial governments to deny aboriginal title and the attempts by Ottawa and Victoria during the late 1800s and into much of this century to frustrate aboriginal peoples' demands for treaties, self-government, and larger reserves. The chapter also discusses the impact of the courts and of some major political events on the province's decision to recognize aboriginal title and to begin a negotiating process that will result in the conclusion of modern-day treaties.

Chapter 2 presents a detailed overview of and a commentary on the major components of the treaty-making process. It includes a discussion of the British Columbia Treaty Commission's function and the six-stage negotiating process. The funding arrangements between the federal and British Columbia governments are also examined, with an emphasis on the cost-sharing agreements affecting pre-treaty, settlement, and implementation costs, including the costs of effecting self-governing arrangements with First Nations. The chapter also presents some reasons why a number of First Nations have decided not to participate in the treaty negotiations, and offers a review of the efforts by governments and some First Nations to open the negotiations to the public and third parties. The chapter concludes with a discussion of the types of interim measures agreements that the province has sought to arrange with First Nations, and the kinds of limitations Victoria has placed on such arrangements.

Chapter 3 presents the reader with an overview of some of the main issues involved in treaty negotiations and, by focusing on the bargaining positions of several aboriginal groups and the federal and British Columbia governments, offers a more in-depth picture of the negotiations. The chapter also contains insights into government positions on lands and resources, the financial benefits that could be offered to First Nations in the treaties, and the nature and scope of forms of aboriginal self-government.

Chapter 4 reviews and addresses the major sources of opposition that have surfaced during the first two years of the treaty talks. It also draws attention to some other issues that should be addressed by all parties as the negotiations mature and move toward the ratification of treaties. The chapter begins by dealing with the most widespread sources of opposition to the talks, namely, the perception of secrecy in the negotiating process and the controversy over the representation of third party interests. The costs associated with treaty-making are also addressed, along with criticisms of the federal and provincial governments' negotiating positions in light of the 1993 British Columbia Court of Appeal decision in *Delgamuukw*. The chapter concludes by raising some questions about the transfer of Crown lands to First Nations, and discusses recent calls for the blanket extinguishment of aboriginal title in the treaties.

Chapter 5 looks at the future of treaty-making in British Columbia. It focuses on the uncertainty that surrounds the process of concluding treaties with aboriginal groups due to Native blockades, the opposition subsequent treaties will face from political forces, and the complaints by some First Nations about the pace with which the negotiations are being conducted. The chapter also considers the possible outcomes of the treaty settlements by posing the following questions and offering some tentative answers to them: Who within the aboriginal community will benefit from the settlements? Will the advantages of treaties be shared by all? Or will they be confined to a select few who hold positions of authority within the new self-governing arrangements that are established? Also, how do we determine whether the treaties meet their desired goals? Could the use of formal analytical methods and the experiences of other jurisdictions involved in land claims provide us with some insights? And, since there is no apparent role for the British Columbia Treaty Commission once the treaties are concluded, how will these settlements be implemented and aboriginal grievances addressed?

The central message of this book is straightforward. There are good reasons for negotiating treaties with aboriginal groups in British Columbia. They are varied and involve the interests of both aboriginal and non-aboriginal people. There are also very good reasons for keeping abreast of the developments in the treaty negotiations and approaching such events with a healthy measure of common sense. No one has to accept without question the views of governments or aboriginal groups involved in the negotiations. Nor should we adopt with blind obedience the perspectives of those who are opposed to the conclusion of treaties. Instead, we should be aware of both sides of the debate and, with a well developed understanding of the Indian land question in British Columbia, arrive at our own conclusions.

As is standard practice in most books on Native issues, a note on the language employed in the following pages is in order. I have used the terms aboriginal peoples, Native peoples, Indians, and indigenous peoples to describe the original inhabitants of British Columbia. All are terms used widely in public debate and none is intended to be used in a pejorative manner. Correspondingly, I have used the terms non-aboriginal, European, and white to describe all others. The same claim to use in a non-pejorative manner applies here as well.

Treaty Talks in British Columbia

1
Prelude to the Treaty-Making Process

To understand the process of treaty-making in British Columbia, and to gain a sense of how non-aboriginal people have arrived at this point in our relationship with the original inhabitants of the province, it is necessary to know something about the aboriginal people of British Columbia, some events of history, and a number of key concepts. Not everyone has to be familiar with all facets of this aspect of the Indian land question in the province; but since the substance of both the negotiations and the final treaty settlements will affect all British Columbians to a greater or lesser extent, it will serve non-Natives well to become knowledgeable, particularly if we are to bring an informed approach to this monumental act of reconciliation.

British Columbia's Aboriginal People

In no other part of North America was the aboriginal population more densely concentrated and culturally diverse than along the coastal areas of present-day British Columbia. While significant populations of Native people resided in other parts of the province – from its northern reaches to its eastern boundary marked by the Rocky Mountains – in sheer numbers and societal differences, they could not match the peoples living along the shores of the Pacific Ocean. To a large extent the uniqueness of the coastal people was the result of geography. With the natural barriers of the Pacific Ocean and the forests and mountains of the Coast Range, those along the coast, while maintaining some contact with their neighbours to the north, remained isolated for the most part, functioning as universes unto themselves. Many groups had their own language and culture, a means of self-identification, and a territory of which they made use. Indeed, similar to indigenous peoples elsewhere in North America, those living along the coast of British Columbia were more culturally diverse than Europeans.[1]

For some time the demographic facts about aboriginal people generally were uncertain. To a large extent they were also deliberately underestimated in order to justify certain myths about Native people or to debase their claims to land.[2] A widely accepted estimate of the pre-contact aboriginal popula-tion in North America was just over one million. Subsequent studies revised this figure upward, with estimates often reaching ten million or more. More recently, these figures have ranged between two and five million.[3] In British Columbia during the 1920s, there were less than 30,000 'status' Indians; however, by 1970 and into the 1980s, the aboriginal population increased steadily. By the mid-1990s approximately 95,000 aboriginal people lived in British Columbia, 45 per cent of whom lived on reserves.[4]

Unlike most 'tribal' societies, the aboriginal communities of the coastal areas of the province had formal institutional structures in which secular authority over civil affairs was vested.[5] They were highly stratified societies, based on rank, status, and hierarchy, and had clearly defined and permanent positions of political leadership. The 'house' or household was the basic social unit: lineages were divided by each house, based on common ancestry. The concept of private property was vital, and just as sophisticated as that of European nations at the time. Each household possessed land for village sites and for hunting and food gathering. Specific items and rights were held in common by the members of each household, including canoes, totem poles, ceremonial objects, and rights to hunt and fish in specific waters and harvest particular food species.[6]

The coastal people built large houses for holding feasts and performances. Such activities were part of the famous potlatches, which performed two main functions. First, they served to legitimize political rank and authority by validating the exercise of chiefly power and influence. Heirs to chieftainship were presented at potlatches, and existing chiefs held potlatches to reaffirm their authority. Food, tools, and clothing were given away as a sign of rank and wealth. Potlatches were vital to maintaining authority. Without them no chief could have assumed his position or maintained it over time. Nor could any individual have been assured of his or her place within a particular house, extended family, or clan. Second, the potlatch ensured the circulation of wealth – and a sort of early-day welfare state – as chiefs maintained their rank and attendant prestige by giving away possessions rather than by retaining them as their own.

While lineage and rank were the organizing principles of coastal peoples, individual equality was the central basis on which the aboriginal people of the interior of British Columbia were organized. Relative to their coastal counterparts, interior communities were small and arranged according to kinsfolk. The absence of major water routes and the need to travel widely made this type of organization almost inevitable. In the northern interior of the province, in the territory of the Sekani and the Tahltan tribal groups, small groups of basically nomadic people were the primary social units. In the southern interior of the province, in the lands of the Kootenay, Okanagan, and Shuswap tribal groups, sedentary winter villages were most common, although occasionally large settlements prevailed, especially in the semi-desert areas surrounding much of the Fraser and Thompson Rivers, where fish and some game were abundant.

Since the aboriginal people of the interior lived in relatively small groups, there was less need for the kind of complex organization that was common along the coast. Yet in some villages with larger populations, permanent chieftainship did exist. For example, among the Okanagan people, chiefly rank could be inherited, and one chief could even be considered the leader of an entire tribal group. But in most cases politics as a specialized activity was not common to the Native peoples of the interior.

The form of politics at the tribal level varied considerably along the Pacific coast and across the interior. Tribal groups consisting of many communities over many territories would have had neither the means nor the incentive for much overall coordination of activities. Those with fewer villages and smaller territories would have been able to communicate more readily, and in cases where adjacent tribal groups were similarly cohesive, there would have been a particular interest in each group maintaining boundaries and acting collectively to protect its interests. However, along the coast, neighbouring aboriginal groups were often invited to potlatches to ensure their awareness of the borders of the various tribes.

Key Concepts Related to Treaties

Aboriginal Rights

Aboriginal rights are based upon the initial occupation of the land by self-governing groups of aboriginal people prior to the arrival of Europeans.[7] As such, aboriginal rights comprise everything necessary to ensure the survival of aboriginal people as aboriginal people, including the right to use and occupy the land and its natural resources, to preserve and foster aboriginal languages and economic and cultural practices, and to practise forms of law and government.

Aboriginal people maintain that these rights continued after European contact and the assertion of British sovereignty. This view is consistent with the common law doctrine of aboriginal rights.[8] The doctrine holds that the Crown's acquisition of land in North America was governed by the principle of continuity. This means that property rights, customary laws, and the various institutions of governance of the aboriginal people were presumed to survive and to be protected by British law. Aboriginal people were able to retain their laws, notwithstanding the presence of English law. Under the principle of continuity, different laws could co-exist. English law was not to be applied retroactively or arbitrarily to the aboriginal people.[9]

The reasoning behind the doctrine of aboriginal rights from the perspective of the colonizing nation is four-fold. First, some recognition of the pre-existing rights of the colonized nation was seen as acceptable and proper, assuming there was no intention to completely annihilate the colonized people. Second, a recognition of pre-existing rights was often necessary in order to exercise effective military control over a particular territory. As will be seen later in this chapter, this reasoning was employed in some of the early treaties concluded between the British Crown and the aboriginal people in the Atlantic region of Canada. These were peace treaties, intended to end warfare. Third, the recognition of pre-existing rights was often necessary to accommodate a previously established and functioning legal system in the territory being overtaken, where it might have been too time consuming and too expensive to remove that system. Fourth, the recognition of pre-existing rights was also a response to various concepts of pluralism by the acquiring state or by international law.[10]

Much of the spirit of the doctrine of aboriginal rights was embodied in the Royal Proclamation of 1763. Issued by King George III of England, and seen by many aboriginal peoples as their Magna Carta, the proclamation was primarily a response to the prospect of war with North American Indians. Consequently, the proclamation set down certain guidelines by which Britain could establish peaceful relations with the aboriginal people. The continuity of land title was explicitly acknowledged in the proclamation's directive to set aside land in North America for aboriginal people, and to reserve it for them as their hunting grounds. The continuity of self-government was implicitly authorized, as well. Indeed, in the treaties concluded between the aboriginal people and the British Crown in other parts of Canada, the continuity of additional aboriginal rights, such as hunting, fishing, and food gathering, was also assured.

Extinguishing Aboriginal Rights

Since its proclamation in 1982, section 35(1) of the Constitution Act of 1982 has recognized and affirmed 'existing' aboriginal rights. If aboriginal rights include those items which are required by aboriginal people to ensure their survival as aboriginal people, how do we determine whether an aboriginal right exists within a particular Native community? And under what conditions can such an aboriginal right be extinguished?

To most legal scholars, in order for an aboriginal right to be seen as 'existing,' there must be some evidence that the aboriginal people concerned possessed and exercised the right at some point in their collective history, and that the right was not extinguished by the Crown prior to 1982. In the 1991 Supreme Court of Canada ruling in *Bear Island*, the Court discussed the criteria that must be satisfied for an aboriginal right to be presumed as 'existing':

- the aboriginal people claiming the right, and their ancestors who purportedly exercised the right, existed as 'organized society'
- this 'organized society' must have occupied a specific territory over which they assert title
- the occupation of the territory was exclusive of any other aboriginal community, and
- the occupation of the territory was an 'established fact at the time British sovereignty was asserted over the land.'[11]

However, assuming that an aboriginal right existed at the time British sovereignty was asserted over the land, there are two ways to determine whether an aboriginal right was extinguished prior to 1982. First, an aboriginal right can be extinguished through a treaty with the Crown. Treaties are therefore very important, for many aboriginal people argue that their rights can be affected only through this mechanism. Consequently, if a treaty does not explicitly refer to certain rights being extinguished, then it should be assumed the right continues to exist. This line of reasoning is consistent with the 'reserved rights doctrine' developed by the courts in the United States, in which an aboriginal right cannot be relinquished unless there was an express intention to do so in the treaty.

Second, the Canadian courts have held that aboriginal rights can be extinguished outside the confines of treaties through legislation enacted prior to 1982. The intention of the legislation to extinguish the right must be 'clear and plain,' either expressly or by 'unavoidable implication,'[12] though the courts have yet to develop a coherent test to determine the clear and plain intention of government.[13] And if the intention of a law was to extinguish an aboriginal right by implication, that is sufficient only if the interpretation of the law permits no other result. Moreover, legislation which is inconsistent with the exercise of an aboriginal right is not sufficient for the right to be extinguished. The 'clear and plain' test is based on the assumption of the role of the Crown as the 'historic protector of aboriginal lands.'[14]

Aboriginal Treaties
A treaty is a solemn agreement between a recognized group or nation of aboriginal people and a representative of the Crown. Treaties are intended

to create obligations for both parties. In most cases aboriginal people agree to forego hostilities or claims relating to land in return for Crown guarantees of protection, game rights, reserve lands, or other benefits. Because a treaty is the result of negotiations between a particular aboriginal group and the government, it is different from an aboriginal right. As noted earlier, aboriginal rights are derived from aboriginal peoples' use and occupation of the land prior to European contact. They are not created by grants, from the government or as a result of governmental negotiations.

Although treaties with First Nations have similarities to both international treaties and contracts, they constitute a separate legal category of a special nature, or *sui generis*. While they are similar to an international treaty in terminology, they do not follow the general rules of international law. Instead, they are considered by government as agreements between the Crown and subjects of the Crown. And unlike international treaties, they can create legal rights even before they are implemented by specific legislation. Similar to contracts, aboriginal treaties are binding legal agreements and they may be subject to the same kind of protections the law applies to contracts. Yet aboriginal treaties involve groups as opposed to individuals, and can prevail over some federal and provincial laws.[15]

The treaties concluded between aboriginal people and the European powers throughout Canada's history come in a variety of forms and reflect the political and economic interests of the parties at the time. Some of the early treaties between the French and aboriginal people took into account French ambitions to colonize New France in order to secure trade and to obtain proof of territorial possession against rival European powers. Aboriginal people entered into these treaties to preserve their territories and their governmental autonomy.[16] Most of these treaties were peace treaties, based on mutual respect, with no subjugation of the aboriginal people or cession of their territory.[17]

Other types of treaties did, however, involve land cession in exchange for cash grants, annuities, and other benefits for the aboriginal people. A requirement of land cession characterized British treaty policy during the post-War of 1812 period, and was seen as a way of securing lands for settlement without engaging in open warfare. The best examples of treaties concluded under these circumstances are the 'numbered treaties,' the majority of which were arranged between 1871 and 1921, covering the Prairie provinces and a section of northeastern British Columbia. Other examples of treaties that involved land cessions were the Robinson treaties in Upper Canada (now Ontario), and the Douglas purchase treaties on Vancouver Island concluded in the 1850s. The last type of treaty is exemplified by the modern land claim agreements in the northern regions of Canada. These treaties involve very large land masses as well as complex governmental, social, and economic institutions and guarantees. They also confer on the aboriginal people modern-day equivalents of the benefits contained in the numbered treaties.[18]

The problems associated with the older types of treaties are numerous. In addition to the remarkable inequity in the bargaining position of the aboriginal treaty-makers vis-à-vis the representatives of the Crown, the treaties were also marred by a series of unfulfilled promises, miserly benefits conferred on aboriginal people, a lack of clarity as to the aboriginal groups subject to the treaty, and often a measure of inappropriateness in many of the treaty guarantees. Moreover, these legal problems were made worse by the unique nature of the treaties. As written agreements, they were foreign to aboriginal oral traditions and, as noted earlier, they occupied a 'middle ground,' somewhere between an international agreement and a domestic contract.

Aboriginal Title

Aboriginal title is a difficult concept to define because it has no counterpart in English property law. It is of a special nature. Nevertheless, aboriginal title can be seen generally as a right of aboriginal people to occupy, use, and enjoy their land and all of its natural resources. It originates in the fact that aboriginal people were in possession of what is now Canada prior to European contact,[19] and it finds support in Canadian law in a variety of legal documents and constitutional structures.[20] Prior to 1982 Canadian law provided that aboriginal title could be regulated and, in some cases, extinguished by legislation.[21] However, since 1982, aboriginal title, like other aboriginal rights, has enjoyed constitutional recognition and protection under section 35(1) of the Constitution Act of 1982. Consequently, any federal, provincial, or territorial law that interferes with the exercise of an aboriginal right must undergo constitutional scrutiny. Furthermore, aboriginal title can be surrendered only to the federal Crown, and only with the consent of the relevant aboriginal community. Once aboriginal title has been extinguished, the federal government may be required to pay compensation to the aboriginal people concerned.[22]

For greater clarity, the courts have described the nature of aboriginal title. As does the definition noted above, early decisions saw aboriginal title as protecting Native people in the 'absolute use and enjoyment of their lands, while at the same time [precluding] them from making any valid alienation [of their land to anyone other] than the Crown itself, in whom the ultimate title was ... vested.'[23] American courts considered aboriginal title to be a set of principles that should be considered just as sacred to aboriginal peoples as the concept of fee simple title is to non-aboriginal people.[24] And more recently, the Supreme Court of Canada defined it as a concept that demonstrated 'the Indian nations were regarded in their relations with the European nations ... as independent nations,'[25] possessing a kind of legal title to their lands.

It must be made absolutely clear that in British Columbia, as in other parts of Canada, the Crown has both underlying and ultimate title to the land. However, because aboriginal title carries with it rights of use and possession, it constitutes a legal burden on the title of the Crown and on its land-related management activities. The Crown's ownership of all the land in British Columbia has never been questioned by the courts or by government. Indeed, aboriginal rights (including aboriginal title) do not supersede Crown title nor call it into question. But the rights of aboriginal people, based on aboriginal title, are such that the underlying title of the Crown is of limited value so long as the burden of aboriginal title remains, as it does in British Columbia, unextinguished. And there is little practical use to which the Crown may put the land so long as aboriginal people retain this interest in the land. As will be seen later in this chapter, these views were articulated by the courts in British Columbia when they issued injunctions halting commercial development in various places in the province. And it is a view that the provincial government eventually came to accept when it decided to lay the foundation for a process by which unextinguished aboriginal title could be dealt with through treaties.

Aboriginal Self-Determination and Self-Government

Aboriginal people assert a right to self-determination on the ground that their survival as distinct collectivities is dependent upon their ability to control the social, cultural, political, and economic issues that affect them. Accordingly, self-determination is considered essential in order for Native people to move away from the colonial mentality of the Indian Act and to break the cycle of dependency of their people on Canadian governments.[26]

Primary to the goal of self-determination is the notion that aboriginal peoples are unique social entities which have been entrusted with the duty of protecting the land and their culture for present and future generations. It has been argued that this traditional duty cannot be adequately discharged in liberal democracies such as Canada because, historically, such systems have neglected aboriginal aspirations and because government policies are often based on the primacy of individual rights, and not collective rights. Neither liberal democracies nor government policies have offered much protection against the assimilation of aboriginal peoples into the mainstream of Canadian society. Only through self-governing structures can aboriginal people hope to achieve a measure of autonomy and self-sufficiency.[27]

Almost all discussions of aboriginal self-determination are rooted in the idea that self-government is considered to be an inherent right accorded to aboriginal people by virtue of their status as the original occupants of the land, whose right to political sovereignty and land entitlement has never been extinguished by treaty or by conquest. Prior to European contact, aboriginal people were organized into politically autonomous structures with sovereign control over their territories. They were never conquered by the French or the English and were generally treated by European nations as independent nations. The recognition and affirmation of aboriginal and treaty rights in section 35(1) of the Constitution Act of 1982 provides a solid legal foundation for aboriginal self-government to become a reality. Yet it remains to be clarified what types of powers self-governing arrangements will afford aboriginal communities, and how these powers will work in tandem with the legislative powers of the federal and provincial governments.

Observers have offered some general comments on the potential function, structure, and jurisdiction of self-governing arrangements. The overall function of aboriginal self-government would be to promote greater self-determination and social justice and to eradicate poverty within aboriginal communities through both economic development and the distribution of wealth. Self-government would also serve to protect aboriginal languages, cultures, and identities, and to provide the means to address policy issues such as housing and health. The structure of aboriginal governments is seen as one that would be distinct and unique from federal and provincial forms of government, and that would be responsible for matters of particular relevance to aboriginal communities. The jurisdiction of self-governing arrangements is expected to vary according to the needs and requests of particular First Nations, but it may include control over the delivery of social services such as education, as well as control over land and natural resources necessary for economic regeneration. Jurisdiction could also include control over aboriginal membership in a particular First Nation and control over the allocation of federal money so that it remains consistent with aboriginal priorities.[28]

The Historical Setting

Early Indian Policy in British Columbia:
James Douglas and the Treaty-Making Process
From the initial point of European contact by Spanish explorers in the sixteenth century, to the time Vancouver Island was declared a colony of Britain in 1849, very little happened to affect the land rights of the aboriginal people. There was some commercial and trading activity between the British and the Native people, but for the most part, the aboriginal people were left undisturbed by the Europeans. Village sites were retained, and traditional hunting and fishing grounds went 'unmolested.'[29]

However, by 1846 British authorities had signed the Treaty of Oregon with the United States, thereby establishing an international border, and in 1849 declared Vancouver Island a British colony. In keeping with the policy of advancing their interests through non-governmental agents, Britain gave the Hudson's Bay Company a grant over the land and its settlement. European settlement in the colony increased. Subsequently, in 1858 Britain proclaimed the Mainland of British Columbia a colony and, during the 1860s, demarcated its eastern and northern borders. Following the unification of the two colonies in 1866, British Columbia joined the Canadian federation as a province in 1871.[30]

From the years 1850 to 1864, James Douglas was the governor of the colony of Vancouver Island. During his tenure he arranged fourteen purchase treaties with the aboriginal people. These treaties were consistent with British policy and with international law at the time. Indeed, one of the first instructions received by Douglas from the Hudson's Bay Company was to negotiate with the chiefs of the tribes of the colony in order to purchase their lands prior to white settlement. Specifically, Douglas was to approach the chiefs on the assumption they were 'the rightful possessors of such lands only as they are occupied by cultivation, or had some houses built on them, at the time when the Island came under the undivided sovereignty of Great Britain in 1846.'[31] The company directed Douglas to consider all other land uncultivated or uninhabited, and therefore available for settlement purposes. It was made clear to Douglas that the aboriginal people in the vicinity would continue to enjoy hunting and fishing rights.

Following his correspondence, Douglas summoned to a conference the chiefs and other representatives of the Songhee, Klallam, and Sooke tribes near present-day Victoria. After some discussion, an arrangement was made whereby the tribes would sell land to the Hudson's Bay Company, except village sites and enclosed fields. After signing an agreement, the tribes would surrender these lands in exchange for some material possessions, the confirmation of their reserves, the right to hunt over unoccupied lands, and the right to carry on fishing activities. As was the preference of the chiefs involved in these initial negotiations, payment for their lands was made in one instalment.[32]

The arrangement made by Douglas stands in contradiction to the instructions given to him by the Hudson's Bay Company: the company directed Douglas to recognize the aboriginal people as possessing only those lands on which their houses stood or around which they had erected fences. The remaining land was considered to be waste, to be used for the purposes of white settlement and for the continued hunting and fishing practices of the aboriginal people.[33] Tennant has attempted to reconcile this contradiction by arguing that the perception of it relies too heavily on the precise wording of the company's instructions rather than on the wording of the treaties themselves. Tennant notes:

> The treaties plainly indicate that Douglas did not regard any land as unowned. The text recognizes each Indian community as initially owning 'whole of the lands' it traditionally occupied. A map of the treaty areas around Fort Victoria shows no gaps between the areas sold by the communities owning them. The starting point for each treaty was that local communities of Indians were recognized as owning every square inch of their traditional lands. It was 'their lands,' excepting their 'Villages Sites and Enclosed Fields,' as Douglas wrote to Barclay and as the treaties stated, that were being sold to the Company.[34]

Tennant's reading of the Douglas treaties is correct but it is also peripheral. Regardless of the content of the treaties he arranged, Douglas still went beyond the scope of the directions of the Hudson's Bay Company. Nevertheless, the treaties arranged by Douglas provide some support for the recognition by imperial and colonial authorities of the pre-existing land rights of the Native people.

The Douglas purchase treaties were comparable to other treaties in Canada and mirrored, to a large extent, those concluded in other parts of the British Empire. The Robinson treaties of Upper Canada included provision for annuities, reserves, and the freedom of the Native people to hunt and fish over unoccupied Crown lands. Except for the provisions involving annuities and the granting of larger reserve lands, the purchase treaties arranged by Douglas contained similar stipulations. Both the Robinson treaties and the Douglas treaties purported to extinguish aboriginal title to large territories, reserving aboriginal title to small tracts. Also, the text of the Douglas treaties was identical to those used by the New Zealand Company when they purchased land from the Maori – only the names, dates, and the amounts to be paid to the various Maori tribes were different.[35]

Between 1850 and 1854 Douglas arranged fourteen purchase treaties on Vancouver Island. Eleven of the treaties cover the areas of Victoria, Sooke, and Saanich. One was concluded at Nanaimo, and two more at Fort Rupert. These last three treaties were intended primarily to acquire coal deposits – the first non-agricultural economic activities undertaken by non-aboriginals in British Columbia. Collectively, the purchase treaties covered approximately 358 square miles (576 square kilometres), or about 3 per cent of the total land mass of Vancouver Island.

It should be pointed out that both British policy and international law of the time set down three methods by which a sovereign nation could acquire additional lands and thus assert its sovereignty. First, land could be acquired through settlement, so long as the land was unoccupied or vacant. This form of territorial acquisition was based on the doctrine of terra nullius. Over time the doctrine was gradually extended to justify the acquisition of inhabited land by occupation, provided the land was not cultivated or its indigenous inhabitants were uncivilized or unorganized into societies permanently united for political action.[36] Second, the land could be acquired through the conquest of the indigenous peoples, in which case the laws and customs of these people would remain in force until altered by the conquering state. Third, the land could be acquired through cession. This method was used in cases where there was a pre-existing society of indigenous peoples holding specific territories subject to cultivation. Acquisition would require the consent of the indigenous peoples to transfer their sovereignty and portions or all of their land to the acquiring state. This new relationship would then be set out in a formal treaty. Those acquiring the sovereignty and the territory were required to pay compensation to those who had ceded it.[37]

In the case of the colony of Vancouver Island, it is clear that the land was occupied by indigenous people prior to European contact and that trading relations between the aboriginal people and the British had carried on for some time. There was no full-scale, armed conflict between the British and the various aboriginal nations. These facts appear to have left Britain only the option of acquiring land and asserting British sovereignty through cession – the approach advocated by the Hudson's Bay Company and followed by Douglas. Indeed, this approach to settlement was acknowledged and endorsed by British authorities. In a letter from Lord Carnavon to Douglas in 1858, the former wrote:

> In the case of the Indians of Vancouver Island and British Columbia, Her Majesty's Government earnestly wish that when the advancing requirements of colonization press upon lands occupied by members of that race, measures of liberality and justice may be adopted for compensating them for the surrender of their territory which they have been taught to regard as their own.[38]

The late Wilson Duff, a well-known anthropologist who undertook studies of the aboriginal people of the Pacific Northwest, noted that the eleven Songhee, Sooke, and Klallam purchase treaties of 1850 contained some irregularities. Douglas arranged the treaties on the assumption that individual families or tribes owned single tracts of land. He failed to account for shared land. For example, the Cheonein (Songhee) were designated as the owners of the lands around Cadboro Bay (directly east of Victoria, north of McNeil Bay, on the eastern side of the Island), and therefore the

Chicowitch (Songhee), who used the land for similar purposes, were not considered owners at all. Moreover, Duff found that in establishing the boundaries of the treaties, Douglas was content to accept the territorial situation of the land as it existed in the 1850s, rather than attempt to reconstruct it to resemble the way it was originally.[39] As will be seen in Chapter 3, these irregularities have resurfaced and are now part of the treaty negotiations involving those First Nations and tribal groups who signed the Douglas treaties.

As Douglas opened up new areas of the colony for settlement, the legislative assembly in Victoria proceeded as if additional treaties were necessary. However, by the late 1850s the practice began to deteriorate. The imperial government revoked the Hudson's Bay Company's grant of Vancouver Island. And although the legislative assembly acknowledged the necessity of treaties with the aboriginal people, the costs of such purchases were felt to be the responsibility of the imperial government. In a letter to the secretary of state for the colonies, Douglas outlined his practice of making treaties with the aboriginal people and asked for the necessary funds to continue to do so:

> As the native Indian population of Vancouver Island have distinct ideas of property in land, and mutually recognize their several exclusive possessory rights in certain districts, they would not fail to regard the occupation of such portions of the Colony by white settlers, unless with the full consent of the proprietary tribes, as national wrongs. Knowing their feelings on that subject, I made it a practice up to the year 1859, to purchase the native rights in the land, in every case, prior to the settlement of any district; but since that time in consequence of the termination of the Hudson's Bay Company Charter, and of the want of funds, it has not been in my power to continue it. Your Grace must, indeed, be well aware that I have, since then, had the utmost difficulty in raising money enough to defray the most indispensable wants of Government.[40]

Despite Douglas's efforts, the British government would not assume any financial obligation for additional treaties. To be sure, the British did not deny the existence of aboriginal title. Nor did they believe that aboriginal lands should not be purchased prior to settlement. Rather, the authorities in London simply believed that they should not have to bear the costs. This was the responsibility of the colonial government in Victoria.

Notwithstanding the stalemate between colonial and imperial authorities, the colonial government in Victoria attempted to purchase aboriginal land. Even Douglas's successor was authorized to spend funds from general revenues for such purposes. However, despite some rather strident public protests and newspaper editorial opinions, which referred to unextinguished aboriginal title as a serious impediment to settlement, no treaties were concluded after 1854.[41] Indeed, it was not until 1899 that another treaty that affected aboriginal lands in British Columbia would be signed. All three layers of governmental authority over the colony – from Britain's Colonial Office, to the governor, to the legislative assembly in Victoria – acknowledged the pre-existing land rights of the aboriginal people. All three placed the onus on the others to resolve the problem. Their efforts were in vain. Nothing was accomplished.

The treaty-making process that was begun by Douglas in the 1850s was now over. In its place came a new process for dealing with the aboriginal people, a process designed to assimilate them into the mainstream of the emerging white society, while fulfilling the overarching goal of land acquisition. This was known later as the 'Douglas system.' It contained three basic strategies. The first two strategies were straightforward and indeed had been used by British authorities for some time in their efforts to colonize distant South Pacific territories.[42] Not only would the aboriginal people be integrated into the British system of education, they would be urged to convert to Christianity. The British saw traditional aboriginal ways of teaching and the aboriginal religion and sense of spirituality as insufficient to prepare the Natives for the new social order, and doing little to advance the 'English element' in the colony.[43]

What was more remarkable was the third strategy. The aboriginal people would be required to settle in villages alongside those established by white settlers. Initially, the villages were to be established on reserves. But since British and colonial officials thought such confinement would undermine the aboriginal peoples' 'pride of independence,' they opted instead to move the aboriginal people and give them the same rights of pre-emption over unsurveyed Crown land as newly arrived immigrants. In short, this was a de facto denial of aboriginal title: there was no mention of the pre-existing land rights of the aboriginal people, no discussion of providing them with some form of compensation for irreclaimable land, and no talk of any negotiations with the aboriginal people over their land. Indeed, the area outside village sites and enclosed fields – the land the Hudson's Bay Company had acknowledged as initially owned by aboriginal people – was now at the disposal of the Crown, to be treated as if it had never been owned.[44]

The Creation of Reserves

Douglas sought to set aside reserves before white settlement occurred so that aboriginal people could maintain villages, agricultural land, and some sacred areas such as burial grounds.[45] This approach was at variance with that used in the United States, where many Native people were removed

from their traditional homes and relocated on large amalgamated reservations. For Douglas, such an approach would only serve to produce hostil-
ity among the aboriginal people – something that was surely not conducive to settlement and peaceful relations. Accordingly, he chose to allow
Native people to select the sites of their reserves, as long as the chosen sites
received the ultimate approval of the district magistrate and were seen as
reasonable and not in conflict with the land sought by white settlers.[46] In
addition, aboriginal people would be allowed to continue using the land
they held at the time, and to use additional arable land, sufficient for growing food.

There is a diversity of views as to the intended size of the allotted
reserves. On one hand, Wilson Duff has claimed that, contrary to Douglas's
suggestion that aboriginal people were to be granted as much reserve land
as they wished and in the areas they desired, the size of the reserves was
calculated on the basis of ten acres per family.[47] On the other hand, Robin
Fisher has noted that the allotment of ten acres per family was regarded as
a minimum.[48] Moreover, in contrast to the reserves established in the
coastal regions of British Columbia, those set aside in the southern interior
were quite large, since many interior aboriginal people could demonstrate
to government officials that their use of land was more extensive by raising horses and cattle. Nevertheless, after Douglas's tenure as governor, ten
acres per family was established as the minimum that was to be used in lay-
ing aside the reserves.

Later Indian Policy in British Columbia:
Joseph Trutch and the Denial of Aboriginal Title

Indian policy in the colony underwent some major changes after Douglas
retired in 1864. In addition to aboriginal title being explicitly denied by
local authorities, many of the reserves established under Douglas's control
were reduced in size. Much of the impetus behind these policy changes
was the result of the imperial government's lack of involvement in the
affairs of the colony. The imperial authorities held little interest in the
colony and indeed in the general welfare of its aboriginal peoples.[49] Support among the English public for the general goals of the British Empire
was on the decline, and both London and the Colonial Office saw little
advantage in shouldering the costs of maintaining a significant interest in
the colony. One result was that much of the control over Indian policy was
left in the hands of local officials, who, while sharing interests with other
white settlers, were now dealing with issues that deeply affected their lives.
It was not surprising, therefore, that the aboriginal people would receive
less than fair treatment by the colonial government in the years to come.[50]

During this time Joseph Trutch emerged as one of the most influential government officials to exercise authority over aboriginal land policy. Unlike Douglas, Trutch considered the aboriginal people 'uncivilized savages' who were ugly and lazy, and prone to lawlessness and violence. No doubt Trutch was a product of Britain's confidence in the superiority of its civilization and its consequent belief that all other races ranked lower on the scale of human existence than the British. Trutch was sceptical about the aboriginal peoples' ability to improve themselves. As opposed to seeing them on an equal footing to white settlers, Trutch saw them as mere obstacles to the development of the colony by the whites.

During his tenure as commissioner of land and works, Trutch made several changes to existing Indian land policy. Under his guidance, in 1866 the colonial legislature prohibited rights of pre-emption by aboriginal people. In areas of white settlement, aboriginal people were restricted to their reserves as far as land use was concerned. Theoretically, this made it possible for a white settler to pre-empt a tract of land larger than a nearby reserve occupied by more than a dozen aboriginal families.[51] Trutch was also the first colonial official of considerable note to deny the application of aboriginal title in the colony. In an 1870 address to the governor, Trutch offered the following words:

> The title of the Indians in the fee of the public lands, or any portion thereof, is distinctly denied. In no case has any special agreement been made with any of the tribes of the Mainland for the extinction of their claims of possession; but these claims have been held to have been fully satisfied by securing to each tribe, as the progress of settlement of the country seemed to require, the use of sufficient tracts of land for their wants of agriculture and pastoral purposes.[52]

Trutch's denial of aboriginal title appears consistent with the de facto denial of aboriginal title on the Mainland of British Columbia, evident in the extension to aboriginal people of the right to pre-empt unsurveyed Crown land. But there was still the problem of the Douglas purchase treaties on Vancouver Island, and their recognition of aboriginal title.[53] Nevertheless, to this Trutch argued that Douglas had arranged

> agreements with the various families of Indians ... for the relinquishment of their possessory claims in the district of the country around Fort Victoria, in consideration of certain blankets and other goods presented to them. But these presents were, as I understand, made for the purpose of securing friendly relations between those Indians and the settlement of Victoria, then in its infancy, and certainly not in acknowledgment of any general title of the Indians to the land they occupy.[54]

Trutch's other alteration to aboriginal land policy was to adjust the boundaries of the reserves established under Douglas's authority. After commencing with the reserve land of the Shuswap people, he made further changes to the size of reserves in the Lower Fraser area. With the concurrence of white settlers and the legislative assembly in Victoria, the reasoning behind the reductions was simple and consistent with Trutch's overall perspective on aboriginal people: they were more bestial than human, and they held lands that they would not and could not develop in a productive way. Such a sentiment was offered by Trutch in his report on the Lower Fraser Indian reserves in August 1867:

> The Indians really have no right to the lands they claim, nor are they of any actual value or utility to them; I cannot see why they should either retain these lands to the prejudice of the general interests of the Colony, or be allowed to make a market of them either to Government or to individuals.[55]

Accordingly, Trutch maintained that every reserve should be adjusted so that aboriginal families received a maximum of ten acres each. And while it has been difficult to determine precisely how much reserve land was removed under Trutch's authority, a report from one of the surveyors at the time noted that such alterations would release for white settlement approximately 40,000 acres.[56]

Trutch's denial of aboriginal title and, in particular, his depiction of the Douglas purchase treaties as mere friendship agreements was not only consistent with the way similar treaties were seen in other jurisdictions subject to British colonialism,[57] but would prove to be remarkably enduring as the colony moved into provincehood. To many non-aboriginal people, Trutch's views were persuasive because they were consistent with their interests and with those of the local government. There was no better way to reinforce non-aboriginal interests in the land than to demonstrate that aboriginal people did not own the land, nor even conceive of owning the land. Continuing Douglas's efforts at treaty-making was pointless: if aboriginal title did not exist, there was no interest in the land that had to be purchased. Furthermore, the reserves set aside for the aboriginal people should not be seen as a recognition of aboriginal title or of the surrender of title to the land adjacent to reserves. Reserves were nothing more than gifts to the aboriginal people from the Crown.[58]

Federal-Provincial Interaction Involving Aboriginal People and the Signing of Treaty Eight

During the discussions surrounding the colony's entrance into the Canadian federation, little time was devoted to the aboriginal people.

Granted, there was a motion that dealt with the types of protection that should be afforded to them during the colony's transition to provincial status, but the motion was ultimately defeated. Although apparently written by Trutch, a clause about aboriginal people was included in the final text of the Terms of Union completely at the insistence of Ottawa.[59]

Clause 13 of the Terms of Union deals with the Native people of British Columbia. It reads:

> The charge of the Indians, and the trusteeship and management of the lands reserved for their use and benefit, shall be assumed by the Dominion Government, and a policy as liberal as that hitherto pursued by the British Columbia Government shall be continued by the Dominion Government after the union.
>
> To carry out such a policy, tracts of land of such an extent as it has been hitherto been the practice of the British Columbia Government to appropriate for that purpose, shall from time to time be conveyed by the Local Government to the Dominion Government in trust for the use and benefit of the Indians, on application of the Dominion Government; and in case of disagreement between the two Governments respecting the quantity of such tracts of land to be so granted, the matter shall be referred for the decision of the Secretary of State for the Colonies.[60]

Whether officials in Ottawa believed the colony's policies on aboriginal people were indeed 'liberal' is a matter of speculation. If anything, there was a considerable measure of confusion among federal politicians as to the substance of the colony's policy on aboriginal people. One politician thought the reserve allotments were similar to those set aside in Ontario, namely, eighty acres per family; another thought the aboriginal people of British Columbia had surrendered their territory through treaties.[61] At any rate, one commentator has suggested that Trutch and other colonial officials were probably less than forthcoming in the information they offered to their federal counterparts, taking pains to assure Ottawa that the colony's aboriginal policy was indeed liberal and generous in the allotment of reserve land and other benefits to the aboriginal people.[62]

After British Columbia entered the Canadian federation in 1871, the federal government assumed direct control and responsibility over the province's aboriginal peoples. Section 91(24) of the Constitution Act of 1867 gave Ottawa legislative jurisdiction in relation to 'Indians, and lands reserved for Indians.' However, the province still held legislative power in other policy fields, which it used to frustrate the ability of Native groups to alter their plight. In 1872 the provincial legislature prohibited aboriginal people from voting in provincial elections, thereby denying them the most fundamental of all democratic rights. And some years later, as a result of the province's title to public lands, provincial officials continued to set aside comparatively small reserves and, in some cases, even reduced the size of established reserves without the consent of the aboriginal residents. Because such acts were within the scope of the province's legislative authority, Ottawa was unable to do much. Ottawa could not force provincial officials to recognize aboriginal title, nor could they motivate the province to increase the size of reserves beyond the required ten acres per family.

Nevertheless, Ottawa's actions in respect of aboriginal people should not go unexamined. In 1876 the federal Parliament enacted the Indian Act, which consolidated existing federal legislation affecting aboriginal people. It was through an amendment to the Act in 1884 that Ottawa outlawed one of the most important political and economic institutions of the coastal people: the potlatch. Moreover, the federal cabinet held constitutional power to disallow any provincial statute.[63] Between the late 1880s and the mid-1940s, almost one-half of all provincial acts disallowed by Ottawa emanated from British Columbia, most of which involved the so-called 'anti-Oriental' laws that had the potential of impeding the construction of the transcontinental railway system. However, during this time the federal cabinet exercised their veto power only marginally in respect of provincial legislation that was detrimental to the interests of aboriginal people. The failure of Ottawa to help or protect aboriginal people was consistent with their overall political priorities. Since Native people occupied such a low place on the scale of political importance, it was more prudent for Ottawa to do very little than to jeopardize healthy intergovernmental relations or alienate a portion of the electorate in British Columbia.

The aboriginal people of the Mainland of British Columbia were not involved in treaty negotiations with the federal government until the late 1890s. With the discovery of gold in the Klondike and the resulting migration toward the Yukon from the Pacific Coast, the federal government was anxious to quash any potential violence as miners and other travellers made their way through aboriginal territory.[64] As one federal official commented at the time:

> The gold seekers plunged into the wilderness of Athabasca without hesitation, and without as much as 'by your leave' to the native. Some of these marauders, as was to be expected, exhibited on the way a congenital contempt for the Indians' rights. At various places his horses were killed, his dogs were shot, his bear-traps broken up. An outcry arose in consequence, which inevitably would have led to reprisals and bloodshed had not the Government stepped in and forestalled further trouble by a prompt recognition of the natives' title.[65]

By 1898 federal officials wasted no time in declaring their intention to make treaties with the aboriginal people in the northern sections of British Columbia. The negotiations were set to commence the following spring.[66]

Federal officials wished first to sign a treaty with those tribes who traded with the Hudson's Bay Company at Fort St. John and Fort Nelson, located in the Peace River District of northeastern British Columbia. While there was some confusion among the aboriginal groups in relation to the date of the proposed signing of the treaty, forty-six Beaver Indians signed an adhesion to Treaty Eight on 30 May 1899, and the remaining members signed additional adhesions to the treaty later.

Similar adhesions were not signed by any other aboriginal group until some years later. Apparently, the treaty commissioners saw little need to obtain adhesions with other aboriginal people until they became troublesome. Moreover, some tribes were reluctant to treat. Some felt that their traditional territory was far too large to sell for the sums offered by the federal government. They also believed that they could survive without the assistance of federal authorities.[67] Nevertheless, other aboriginal groups seemed eager to treat, and on 15 August 1910, the Slave and Sekani tribes signed an adhesion to Treaty Eight.[68]

As was the standard practice of the time, the provisions of Treaty Eight reflect a recognition by the federal commissioners that the aboriginal signatories could continue their traditional economic activities, such as fishing and hunting, over unoccupied Crown land.[69] Designated tracts of land were surrendered by the aboriginal people in exchange for an allotment of one square mile (1.61 square kilometres) for each family of five. Initial cash payments were given to the chiefs and councillors of the various tribes, and provision was made for education, farm stock, implements, and ammunition. It should be noted, however, that the process of bringing the aboriginal people formally into Treaty Eight was rather haphazard. For the most part, federal officials were ignorant of the nomadic lifestyle of the aboriginal people,[70] and there is evidence to suggest that the federal government intended to sign treaties with additional tribes in British Columbia but failed to do so.

The government of British Columbia played no significant role in the conclusion of Treaty Eight. Not only did the province have little, if any, 'official' presence in the area, but the belief that the province held clear title to the land, unencumbered by aboriginal title, was firm. As aboriginal title was viewed as immaterial, so was the need to conclude treaties with Native groups. In addition, federal officials were well aware of the province's position in this regard, and knew that any hope of seeing the province participate in the negotiations, either by setting aside reserve lands or by bearing some of the costs of the negotiations, was fruitless.

However, the federal government was able to work around the provincial reluctance to relinquish land for reserves by setting aside a parcel of land known as the 'Peace River Block' – a 5,500-square-mile (8,855-square-kilometre) section of land that was previously conveyed by the province to the federal government for railway and agricultural purposes.[71]

That the federal government was able to conclude a treaty without the involvement of British Columbia is significant for present-day treaty negotiations in British Columbia. Some have argued that the provincial government should not and need not participate in the negotiations. In addition to the costs of doing so, there is little constitutional authority for the province to act in such negotiations. Constitutional authority over 'Indians, and lands reserved for Indians' is assigned to the federal government, with no corresponding legal responsibility attached to the provincial government. If there is no legal requirement for the province to arrange treaties, why, then, should it be engaged in a treaty-making process? Could not the experiences of Treaty Eight be used to support the argument for concluding treaties with aboriginal groups in British Columbia without the involvement of the provincial government?

To accept this argument as realistic, we would need to make several assumptions. The first is that there is enough federally owned land in British Columbia for treaty settlements; second, that these lands hold sufficient commercial potential to allow the aboriginal economic development initiatives that may be included in some of the treaties to be viable; and third, that the provincial government wishes to play no role in the development of Native communities or industries, nor share in the benefits that may flow from such development. Not only is the plausibility of these assumptions doubtful; but the exclusion of the provincial government from the treaty negotiations would suggest a replication of the conditions on which the adhesions to Treaty Eight were signed: the provincial government denied that aboriginal title existed in British Columbia; there was little provincial involvement in the areas subject to treaty negotiations; and aboriginal people and non-aboriginal people existed largely independent of each other, with little contact between their respective communities. Surely, these conditions do not apply to British Columbia today; and the argument that the province should refrain from participating in treaty talks should therefore be rejected as an unrealistic conception of contemporary circumstances.

Aboriginal Protests

The legislative enactments of both Ottawa and Victoria induced aboriginal people to take a more direct and confrontational approach to their dealings with government. In 1872 a number of chiefs of the Coast Salish tribes of the Lower Fraser River rallied in front of the provincial land registry office in New Westminster, demanding the enlargement of the existing reserves. In 1881 a delegation of Nisga'a travelled to Victoria, also demanding additional reserve land. Several years later a number of Tsimshian chiefs led a delegation to Ottawa. They met with Prime Minister John A. Macdonald, who gave the chiefs his reassurance that the issue of insufficient reserve land would be addressed.[72]

However, such forms of protest appeared to accomplish very little in substantive terms. By the late 1880s, the dissatisfaction among the aboriginal people reached new heights, manifesting itself in other acts of protest. Both Nisga'a and Tsimshian refused to allow provincial land surveyors into their traditional territories. Several Tsimshian openly expressed a desire to move their members to Alaska, where it was reported the United States would offer them a more generous land policy. And news of the Okanagan and Shuswap tribes forming a confederacy to assert their claims to additional land began to cause anxiety among government officials and white settlers.[73]

The provincial government appeared sufficiently motivated by these events for Premier William Smithe to meet with the chiefs of the Nisga'a and Tsimshian during the early months of 1887. The chiefs demanded additional reserve land, treaties, and self-government. Smithe, however, refused to take their entreaties seriously, suggesting that such talk of treaties and self-government was nothing more than a disguised plea for more land. Indeed, just after characterizing the aboriginal people prior to European contact as 'little more than wild beasts of the field,' Smithe offered a rebuttal to the chiefs' view of land ownership with the following words:

> The land all belongs to the Queen ... A reserve is given to each tribe, and they are not required to pay for it. It is the Queen's land just the same, but the Queen gives it to her Indian children because they do not know so well to make their own living the same as the white man, and special indulgence is extended to them, and special care shown. Thus, instead of being treated as a white man, the Indian is treated better. But it is the hope of everybody that in a little while the Indians will be so far advanced as to be the same as a white man in every respect.[74]

In the face of such recalcitrance by the provincial government and the unabated progress of white settlement throughout the province, aboriginal groups began to develop new forms of political organization. In 1916 various coastal and interior groups formed the first province-wide aboriginal political organization: the Allied Tribes of British Columbia (ATBC). The ATBC lobbied both the federal and provincial governments for additional reserve land and for treaties. But perhaps more significantly, since it marked the beginning of a new strategy for aboriginal groups in their relations with government, the ATBC threatened litigation as a means of advancing their goals. The reasoning behind the decision to pursue the recognition of aboriginal rights in court was straightforward. It seemed clear after many years that negotiations between aboriginal people and both orders of government were going nowhere. The rights of aboriginal people in the province continued to be restricted. And despite aboriginal protests, both governments were working together to reduce the size of reserve lands.[75] For the ATBC, litigation would remove their demands from the political forum and place them in the legal arena, where there seemed to be a greater chance they would receive a fair and objective hearing. A judicial decision recognizing the continuing existence of aboriginal title in the province would draw attention to the illegality of many of the actions of the provincial government since at least Trutch's time and represent a significant bargaining chip for the aboriginal people in their subsequent negotiations with government. Indeed, the attractiveness of using litigation increased when the Judiciassl Committee of the Privy Council, in a 1921 case arising in Nigeria, ruled that aboriginal title was a pre-existing right that must be presumed to survive, unless established otherwise by the context or the circumstances in which the right operated.[76] Thus, if an analogous claim from British Columbia could reach the Judicial Committee, then there might be a good chance the law lords would offer a similar ruling.

The ATBC would continue their operations for only about a decade. Due largely to a series of amendments to the Indian Act, the goals of the ATBC were severely limited. In 1884 Ottawa amended the Act's provisions prohibiting the potlatch to extend to many aboriginal ceremonies and activities which involved the exchange of goods, material, or money. In addition – and probably as a result in part of the Judicial Committee's ruling on the pre-existence of aboriginal title – the federal government made a further amendment to the Indian Act in 1927 that prohibited any aboriginal group from raising funds to support claim-related activities, without the government's consent. This provision would remain in effect until 1951.

Despite the efforts by government to suppress aboriginal political and legal activities, another political organization emerged in 1931 in the wake of the ATBC: the Native Brotherhood of British Columbia (NBBC). Grouping the interests of the north and central coast peoples, the NBBC continued the ideals of the ATBC. But they also sought to broaden the scope of their concerns. The NBBC advocated improvements to the level of education among aboriginal people, greater recognition in law of their hunting, fishing, and logging rights, and the decriminalization of the potlatch. Notwithstanding the Indian Act's prohibition on claims activity, the NBBC remained steadfast in their insistence on government recognition of aboriginal title. The NBBC effectively performed the role of liaison between their constituency and government officials, assisting individual members in their interaction with government and holding forums in which various concerns could be raised. Yet the overall effectiveness of the NBBC was limited by their inability to forge a province-wide alliance with tribal groups on the south coast and in the interior of the province.[77]

As time wore on, other aboriginal political organizations would emerge in the province. Some organizations, such as the Nisga'a Tribal Council, and later the Nuu'Chah'Nulth Tribal Council, arose from the remnants of the NBBC, and sought to work toward the resolution of their land claims. Others, such as the North American Indian Brotherhood, were comprised of various aboriginal groups from the interior and the southern coast who also sought the recognition of aboriginal title by government, but held additional concerns about the socio-economic status of aboriginal people, as well as the restrictions placed upon aboriginal development and self-determination by the Indian Act and the administration of Indian affairs. Still others, like the Confederation of Native Indians of British Columbia, provided a forum for coordinating the activities of other aboriginal organizations, with a view to uniting their common interests. Collectively, these organizations would respond to governmental initiatives and serve as political forums that reflected aboriginal understandings, perceptions, and identities.[78]

The Role of the Courts, and Federal and Provincial Policy Responses

The willingness of various aboriginal political organizations to resort to litigation would do much to induce changes to both federal and provincial policies concerning aboriginal title in those areas of Canada where formal treaties did not exist. Indeed, from the early 1970s to the early 1990s, various judicial decisions would not only cause such changes, but would give aboriginal people a solid foundation on which their subsequent negotiations with both orders of government could proceed.

One of the most important cases affecting aboriginal title in British Columbia was the 1973 Supreme Court of Canada decision in *Calder*.[79] Frank Calder was a hereditary chief of the Nisga'a and the member of the provincial legislature for Atlin. Calder was instrumental in the formation of the Nisga'a Tribal Council. Among his notable accomplishments was his effort to obtain a declaration from the courts that aboriginal title was still in effect in British Columbia. The legal argument put forward by the Nisga'a was two-fold: they argued first that the Nisga'a held aboriginal title to their ancient tribal lands in the Nass Valley prior to the assertion of British sovereignty; and second, that such title had not been lawfully extinguished. Therefore, the Nisga'a claimed, they still held aboriginal title to these lands.

Initially, the case was heard by the British Columbia Supreme Court. Counsel for the provincial government responded to the Nisga'a argument by asserting that aboriginal title did not exist in British Columbia because the Royal Proclamation of 1763 (which, for the province, was the source of aboriginal title) did not apply to the province. For aboriginal title to have meaning and application in the province, it had to have been created explicitly by imperial authorities at the time British sovereignty was asserted over the land. Moreover, the province's lawyers argued that even if aboriginal title had existed in British Columbia before the assertion of sovereignty, it had been extinguished implicitly prior to 1871 by colonial land legislation.

While both the British Columbia Supreme Court and later the British Columbia Court of Appeal upheld the province's legal argument, the Supreme Court of Canada granted leave to the Nisga'a to appeal the rulings. Here the result was somewhat different, although the appeal was ultimately dismissed by the Court. Six justices found that the Nisga'a held aboriginal title before the assertion of British sovereignty. However, on the question of whether aboriginal title continued to exist in the province, the justices were split evenly: three held that aboriginal title continued to exist; three ruled that, while aboriginal title may have existed, it was extinguished by the assertion of British sovereignty and implicitly by colonial actions prior to 1871. Moreover – and this was the reason for the appeal's dismissal – four of the seven justices found that the Nisga'a had improperly brought the suit before the Court, since they had failed to obtain a fiat from the British Columbia government to do so.

Nevertheless, the Supreme Court ruling was sufficiently divided to induce the federal government to adopt a new policy on aboriginal title. Prior to the ruling in *Calder*, the federal government's aboriginal policy was not clearly defined. In 1969 Ottawa introduced the White Paper, which sought the eventual elimination of the various 'privileges' of aboriginal people, with the ultimate goal of 'normalizing' their integration into Canadian society. Among other things, the White Paper would have done away with the Indian Act, phased out federal obligations to aboriginal people, and parcelled out reserve land on the basis of individual ownership. However, the White Paper was condemned by almost all aboriginal groups as racist in intent, and a form cultural genocide. In 1971 the federal government withdrew it. In its place Ottawa established the Core Funding Program, which provided aboriginal groups with the resources necessary for the promotion of their causes through research, legal channels, and publicity.[80] But it was not until the 1973 *Calder* ruling that a common ground emerged between Ottawa and the Native community. The federal government then began a process of treaty-making in the north, and commenced negotiations with the Nisga'a over land in the Nass Valley. Indeed, former prime minister Trudeau, in recounting the Supreme Court's decision and its policy implications, remarked that the case pushed him to reconsider the colonialist assumptions underlying his administration's policy on aboriginal people, and to acknowledge the possibility of aboriginal self-determination, treaty rights, and self-government as key organizing principles.[81]

In 1984 the Supreme Court of Canada went further in recognizing aboriginal title as an established legal right in Canadian law. Following their earlier finding in *Calder*, the Court's majority ruled in *Guerin* that aboriginal peoples' interest in their lands was a pre-existing legal right not created by the Royal Proclamation of 1763, but rather derived from the historic occupation and possession by aboriginal people of their tribal lands. Consequently, pre-existing aboriginal title was still a valid legal right on reserve land in British Columbia and on traditional tribal lands not subject to treaties with the Crown.[82]

After *Guerin*, the courts seemed for many aboriginal groups to be the most effective vehicle by which to advance their interests against those of government. Within several weeks of the *Guerin* ruling, the Nuu'Chah'-Nulth nations blocked access to MacMillan Bloedel's timber berth on Meares Island. While Meares Island was not reserve land, the chiefs of the Clayoquot and Ahousaht First Nations sought a declaration from the courts that any provincial permit which allowed logging or in any other way interfered with aboriginal title on Meares Island was beyond the powers of the provincial government. They applied to a British Columbia Supreme Court judge for an injunction to halt logging until this claim had been resolved at trial. Central to this application was the desire to preserve evidence of the aboriginal peoples' historic use of the natural resources of the area. The province countered the claim by insisting again that aboriginal title to the land had been extinguished by colonial land legislation prior to 1871. MacMillan Bloedel argued that economic chaos would prevail if the injunction was granted by the Court.

The British Columbia Supreme Court rejected the chiefs' legal argument and thus rejected the application for an injunction. The chiefs appealed to the British Columbia Court of Appeal. The Court was divided three to two in favour of granting the injunction. Justice Seaton gave one of the majority judgments:

> The [British Columbia Supreme Court] judge thought the claim to Indian title so weak that he could safely conclude that it could not succeed. I do

not agree with that view ... The proposal is to clear-cut the area. Almost nothing will be left. I cannot think of any native right that could be exercised on lands that have been recently logged ... I am firmly of the view that the claim to Indian title cannot be rejected at this stage of the litigation ... The Indians have pressed their land claims in various ways for generations. The claims have not been dealt with at all. Meanwhile, the logger continues his steady march and the Indians see themselves retreating into a smaller and smaller area. They, too, have drawn the line at Meares Island. The island has become a symbol of their claim to rights in the land ... It is too important to the Indians' case that they be able to show their use of this forest. I do not mean to suggest that the Indians ought to continue to use the forest as they used it in the past. The importance of the evidence of extensive use is that it may demonstrate a right to continued use ... It has ... been suggested that a decision favourable to the Indians will cast a huge doubt on the tenure that is the basis for the huge investment that has been and is being made. I am not influenced by that argument ... There is a problem about tenure that has not been attended to in the past. We are being asked to ignore the problem as [the province of British Columbia has] ignored it. I am not willing to do that.[83]

The Court was also explicit in its judgment of what was expected of the provincial government. According to Justice MacFarlane:

The fact that there is an issue between the Indians and the province based upon aboriginal claims should not come as a surprise to anyone. Those claims have been advanced by the Indians for many years. They were advanced in [the *Calder* case], and half the court thought they had some substance ... *I think it is fair to say that, in the end, the public anticipates that the claims will be resolved by negotiations and by settlement.* This judicial proceeding is but a small part of the whole process which will ultimately find its solutions in a reasonable exchange between governments and the Indian nations.[84] (emphasis added)

After *Martin*, the British Columbia Supreme Court issued injunctions to many First Nations whose claims had not been heard. As a result, logging was halted on Deer Island in Kwakiutl territory, further railway development was prevented along the Thompson River, and logging preparation was enjoined in the Gitxsan and Wet'suwet'en territory. These injunctions prevented the province from treating the land as though aboriginal title did not exist, and they also prompted the major natural resource development companies to consider whether their own interests would not be better served if the province entered into treaty negotiations with First Nations.[85]

One of the results of *Martin* was the creation of the provincial Ministry of Native Affairs in 1988. Judicial support for the claims of aboriginal groups induced the new Social Credit government to entertain a more accommodating policy on aboriginal issues than earlier provincial governments. Yet, like their predecessors, the government still refused to acknowledge aboriginal title and to enter into treaty negotiations with the First Nations. Despite this, several events would work in tandem to force a change in the government's position. By 1989 public support for treaties hit approximately 80 per cent, as public knowledge about land claims increased.[86] Several conferences involving representatives of tribal groups and senior officials in the natural resource sector produced a consensus of opinion that treaty negotiations may be necessary if the development of the province's resource sector was to continue unimpeded.

Under these conditions, the new minister of Native affairs, Jack Weisgerber, along with his deputy minister, Eric Denhoff, approached the provincial cabinet and suggested that negotiations with First Nations might be the best course of action for the government to pursue. After touring the province to meet with a number of First Nations, Premier Vander Zalm appointed a Native affairs advisory committee to consider the government policy options. In time, a number of the committee's members declared their support for negotiations, and it seemed likely this would be the policy position recommended to the premier.[87] Soon after, Native blockades were erected at Oka and at Kahnawake, not far from Montreal, creating a spillover effect across Canada, particularly in Alberta and British Columbia.[88] Various aboriginal groups in these provinces set up their own blockades, both in support of the Mohawk claims to land and to draw attention to their specific grievances with government. Vander Zalm visited a number of the blockades in British Columbia and addressed the protesters. By the fall of 1990, the premier announced that his government would commence negotiations with First Nations. But still he refused to acknowledge aboriginal title in the province.

Delgamuukw

In 1987 the Gitxsan and Wet'suwet'en tribal nations launched a legal action in the British Columbia Supreme Court. Their claim was for a right of ownership and jurisdiction to more than 22,000 square miles (35,420 square kilometres) of their traditional territory on the grounds that no part of it had been ceded to or purchased by the Crown. The pre-existing land rights of the Gitxsan and Wet'suwet'en people remained therefore unextinguished. In March of 1991 the Court delivered its judgment. Chief Justice McEachern rejected the claim. In dealing with the two sources of aboriginal title, the Royal Proclamation of 1763 and the common law, the chief justice found that the Proclamation did not apply to British Columbia, since the colony did not fall within the territories contemplated by the language of the document. The extent of the North American continent was simply unknown in 1763. As regards the common law, although the chief justice left the scope of aboriginal rights largely undefined through a review of some recent cases, he found that they arose through the occupation and use of the specific lands for aboriginal purposes for an indefinite, long period of time prior to British sovereignty. However, after considering a series of colonial enactments, he found that such interests had been extinguished implicitly when the Crown exercised complete dominion over the territory by opening the land to settlement prior to 1871.[89]

Justice McEachern's ruling was castigated by First Nations and by many members of the academic and legal communities. Leave to appeal to the British Columbia Court of Appeal was granted, and in June 1993 the Court rendered its decision.[90] The Court's majority rejected Justice McEachern's view that all the aboriginal rights of the Gitxsan and Wet'suwet'en people had been extinguished prior to 1871. Howevser, the majority were careful to make it clear that those aboriginal rights that do remain do not entail the unfettered right to use, occupy, and control the lands and their resources. On the question of jurisdiction, which amounted to a claim to a right of self-government, the Court's majority held that such powers would constitute legislative powers that could encroach upon those of the federal and provincial governments. Consequently, not only would powers of this sort be inconsistent with the legislative powers laid down in sections 91 and 92 of the Constitution Act of 1867, but they would run contrary to the principle of parliamentary supremacy. In short, the Court found that it held 'no power to make grants of constitutional authority in the face of clear and comprehensive statutory and constitutional provisions,'[91] and that no group could make rules which derogated from an act of Parliament.

Despite these findings, and doubtless as an affirmation of the current treaty-making process currently under way in British Columbia, both the Court's majority and dissenting opinions suggested that negotiations between First Nations and the federal and provincial governments would be the best method of determining the nature and scope of the aboriginal rights still in existence. Indeed, the Court's emphasis on a resolution of these issues through negotiations also extended to that 'form of Indian self-government [which could operate] beyond the regulatory powers of the Indian Act,' and which could co-exist with 'other levels of government.'[92]

2
The Process of Treaty-Making

With the announcement by Premier Vander Zalm of the provincial government's intention to negotiate with First Nations, the First Nations
Congress (later named the First Nations Summit) responded by organizing
two meetings with officials from both federal and provincial levels of government. One meeting was held with Prime Minister Brian Mulroney, the
other with Premier Vander Zalm. Representatives of all First Nations in the
province were invited to attend. The meetings were conducted in a spirit of
cooperation, and new approaches toward resolving the land question were
discussed. Mulroney was willing to change the present federal comprehensive claims process so that more than one claim could be addressed con-
currently. However, the First Nation representatives were somewhat
guarded. Except for some of the Nisga'a representatives, none of the First
Nations had previous experience in treaty negotiations with the federal or
British Columbia governments. None wished to be caught without a
thoughtful, strategic position, or put into a position where they could be
outflanked by more skilled government negotiators. Therefore the First
Nations Congress suggested the creation of a tripartite task force to recom-
mend appropriate procedures and principles on which to base the negotiations. Both governments agreed to the suggestion. On 3 December 1990,
the British Columbia Claims Task Force was established.

The task force consisted of appointees from all three parties. The federal
government appointed two representatives. One appointee was Murray
Coolican, a consultant and the former chairman of an earlier federal task
force designed to review Ottawa's land claims policy. Coolican was also an
expert on treaties. The other federal appointee was Audrey Stewart, an official with the Department of Indian Affairs and Northern Development,
with considerable experience in negotiating specific claims. British
Columbia also made two appointments to the task force. Tony Sheridan
was the deputy minister of Native affairs and had been with the provincial

government for almost three decades, holding a variety of positions in the Ministry of the Attorney General. The other provincial appointee was Allan Williams, a Vancouver lawyer, former minister of labour, and former attorney general of British Columbia. The First Nations Summit appointed three individuals. The first was Chief Joe Mathias, a hereditary chief of the Squamish First Nation, who held a number of advisory positions on boards and committees at the regional level in Vancouver. The second appointee was Chief Edward John, a lawyer and a hereditary chief of the Carrier-Sekani First Nation. The third appointee was Miles Richardson, president of the Council of the Haida Nation.[1]

The task force considered the historical background of early treaty-making in British Columbia and other parts of Canada, and covered the issues that should be subject to treaty negotiations, as well as a process for the negotiations. It consulted with a number of individuals and organizations and received submissions from a wide variety of interests. In the end, the task force put forward nineteen recommendations.[2]

On 21 September 1992, representatives of the First Nations Summit and the federal and British Columbia governments made a formal commitment to negotiate modern-day treaties by signing the British Columbia Treaty Commission Agreement.[3] The agreement endorsed all of the nineteen recommendations put forward by the Claims Task Force. Two of its most significant recommendations were to set up the British Columbia Treaty Commission and establish a six-stage treaty negotiation process.

The British Columbia Treaty Commission
The British Columbia Treaty Commission (henceforth referred to as the commission) was appointed on 15 April 1993, and labelled as the 'keeper of the process.' It functions as an impartial and independent tripartite body, designed to assist in facilitating the treaty negotiations by monitoring developments and by providing, when necessary, methods of dispute resolution. The commission also allocates funding to First Nations for their negotiations. The commission consists of five commissioners: two appointed by First Nations; one from each order of government; and a chief commissioner agreed to by each of the three principals. A report on the effectiveness of the process and on the progress of each negotiation is undertaken by the commission and delivered to the public, to both orders of government, and to First Nations.[4] The First Nations Summit passed a resolution indicating their approval of the role of the commission, and British Columbia enacted legislation for the same purpose. At the time of writing the federal government has yet to signal its legislative approval of the commission.

The Process of Treaty-Making

The treaty-making process is conducted entirely on a voluntary basis: no First Nation is compelled to enter into negotiations with the federal and British Columbia governments. Up to stage four of the six-stage process, negotiators from any of the parties are free to introduce into the talks any issue deemed worthy of inclusion. The six stages of the treaty-making process are as follows.

Stage One: Statement of Intent

The treaty-making process begins once a First Nation files with the commission a Statement of Intent (SOI) to negotiate a treaty. Once the commission accepts an SOI as complete, it is submitted to the federal and provincial governments. For the SOI to be complete, it must identify the First Nation proposing to negotiate a treaty, along with the people that First Nation represents. The First Nation must also describe the area of its traditional territory, and it must indicate a formal contact person for subsequent communication between the parties.

Stage Two: Preparations for Negotiations

Within forty-five days of receiving an SOI, the commission is required to convene a meeting with the three parties. Often held in the traditional territory of the relevant First Nation, this initial meeting allows the parties and the commission to exchange information, consider the criteria that will determine the parties' readiness to negotiate a treaty, discuss the research that may be undertaken in preparation for the negotiations, and identify in a general fashion the main issues of concern to each of the parties.

After this initial meeting, the parties begin readying themselves for the third stage of the process. The commission determines the extent to which the parties are prepared to begin the negotiation of a Framework Agreement. Each party must have the following items in place:

- an appointed negotiator, with a clear mandate to negotiate
- sufficient resources to carry out the negotiations
- a ratification procedure
- an identification of both the substantive and procedural issues to be negotiated.

More specifically, at this stage each First Nation must have indicated a process for resolving any issues involving overlapping territory with neighbouring First Nations. The federal and British Columbia governments must have obtained not only some background information on the negotiating aboriginal community, its people, and the non-aboriginal interests that could be affected by the negotiations within the claim area, but they must also have a mechanism for consulting with non-aboriginal and third party interests.

Once the commission determines that the above criteria have been satisfied, it will confirm that the parties are prepared to begin the third stage of the process: the negotiation of a Framework Agreement.

Stage Three: Negotiation of a Framework Agreement

The Framework Agreement is essentially a negotiated agenda that identifies the issues to be negotiated, the goals of the negotiation process, any special procedural arrangements, and a timetable for the negotiations. At the time of writing, only a few negotiations had reached this stage of the process, the Sechelt nation being the first to complete it.

Stage Four: Negotiation of an Agreement in Principle

The substantive negotiations begin at this stage of the process, arriving at a series of agreements that will form the basis for the treaty. The Agreement in Principle will also establish the ratification procedure for each party to the negotiations and be submitted to the relevant constituents for their approval, rejection, or amendment. The British Columbia government has indicated that Agreements in Principle will be subject to public review before ratification. The completion of this stage of the process provides the parties with a mandate to conclude a treaty.

Stage Five: Negotiation to Finalize a Treaty

The treaty that is concluded at this stage of the process will formalize the relationship between the parties and embody the agreements reached in the Agreement in Principle. Certain issues of a legal or technical nature will be resolved at this stage, and those issues already settled will not be reopened. At the completion of this stage, a Final Agreement will be signed and formally ratified.

Stage Six: Implementation of the Treaty

Plans for the long-term implementation of each of the treaties will be made during this stage of the process.

Funding the Treaty-Making Process

Funding provisions for all stages of the treaty-making process, from negotiation to implementation, were established in a Memorandum of Understanding (MOU) between the federal and British Columbia governments, dated 21 June 1993.[5] The MOU is divided into three parts.

Part One: Pre-Treaty Costs, Settlement Costs, and Implementation Costs

Responsibilities of the Parties

The MOU begins by setting forth the responsibilities of the federal and British Columbia governments to each other and to the First Nations involved in the process. The governments agree to provide lands and resources (including financial resources) to conclude treaties. This includes bearing the costs of negotiating with First Nations, and sharing research and information. The governments also have a responsibility to First Nations to undertake joint public education programs, to share and exchange information, to manage the costs of the negotiations effectively, and to establish a process whereby the concerns of groups directly affected by treaties are considered during the negotiations. However, unless there is a prior agreement between the governments, each agrees not to propose or conclude a treaty provision that would, if implemented, result in the other government assuming additional financial or other obligations. In short, the MOU prohibits one government from off-loading treaty costs onto the other government.[6]

Pre-Treaty Costs

The costs of certain pre-treaty items are borne by the federal and British Columbia governments, in a 60 per cent-40 per cent breakdown, respectively. This cost-sharing formula includes the costs of the commission's activities, third party consultation and advisory structures, public information programs, and ratifying the treaties by the First Nations. The same funding formula is applied to certain 'land information systems' that will determine the costs of identifying: any claim overlaps, current land use and land use planning processes, renewable and non-renewable natural resources, and land subject to third party interests. Third party interests are defined in the MOU as: 'existing legal interests, rights, permits, leases or licences respecting lands and resources, or both, which are held by third parties.'[7]

The federal government is to absorb the total costs of the loans made to First Nations to participate in treaty negotiations. However, this commitment is subject to two conditions: (1) If a First Nation defaults on the repayment of a loan, within two years of the default the British Columbia government is required to pay the federal government 50 per cent of the amount of principal due, and 50 per cent of the amount of interest accrued and due at the time the Agreement in Principle was signed with the First Nation. (2) If a First Nation has paid an amount to rectify a loan in default, the federal government will reimburse British Columbia an amount equal to 50 per cent of any amount paid by the First Nation in partial default of a loan.[8]

Settlement Costs

The MOU divides settlement costs into three categories: cash, the costs of purchasing third party interests to conclude treaties, and provincial Crown lands provided to First Nations to conclude a treaty. (1) Cash costs include capital transfers to First Nations for settlement purposes; resource revenues lost to either government as a result of treaties; and the market value of any urban or exceptional forest land, and non-urban federal land provided through treaties. While cash allotments will be shared evenly by both governments, the primary responsibility will rest with the federal government. A formula for determining each government's share of cash has been established, but as the ratio of provincial Crown land increases, the province's share of cash will decrease. Official documents indicate that the provincial contribution of cash will range between 10 per cent and 25 per cent. (2) Third party interests may be purchased to conclude treaties. The costs of doing so will be shared evenly by the federal and British Columbia governments. (3) Land costs pertain to Crown land transferred to a First Nation. But the MOU notes that urban land, exceptional quality forest land, non-urban federal land, and resource revenue lost to either government will be treated as cash equivalents. The main responsibility for the provision of Crown land lies with the British Columbia government.[9]

Implementation Costs

The MOU addresses adjustment costs, which may arise in circumstances where the provincial government is required to provide additional financial assistance to communities, municipalities, and to individuals adversely affected by treaties. The federal government will pay for such costs at the rate of $3 million (1993 dollars) at the conclusion of each treaty, until all of the treaties have been concluded, or until the net present value of all payments reaches $40 million, whichever comes first.[10]

Part Two: Self-Government Costs

Responsibilities

The duties of the governments for bearing the costs of self-government include providing the financial resources required to reach agreements on self-government in a timely and effective manner. Each government is obligated to bear its own costs of negotiating such agreements; to share and exchange information; and to undertake with First Nations joint public education programs. As in other parts of the treaty-making process, each government must establish some process for consultation with groups directly affected by aboriginal self-government to ensure their concerns are considered during negotiations.[11]

Expenditures for Cost-Sharing

Similar to the cost-sharing formula for pre-treaty and settlement costs, the breakdown of federal and provincial government responsibilities for the costs of developing First Nations self-governing arrangements is 60 per cent and 40 per cent, respectively. The same cost-sharing arrangement will apply to joint party consultation, to public information programs, and to the participation of First Nations in the negotiations.[12]

The MOU indicates that aboriginal self-government can include law-making and administrative powers. Consequently, in the development of core institutions of self-government, the federal government is obligated to bear all such costs. All other costs associated with self-government programs and services will be subject to negotiation between the two orders of government. However, if over time, under a particular self-governing arrangement, the fiscal capacity of a First Nation reaches a stage where a reduction in funding by both governments is warranted, the savings will be shared by the governments in the same proportion as funding was provided initially. The mechanism by which funds are transferred to First Nations for self-governing arrangements will be negotiated between both governments and the relevant First Nation. Capital transfers will likely take the form of block grants.[13]

Part Three: Implementation of the Memorandum of Understanding

The 'effectiveness and efficiency' of the cost-sharing agreements in the MOU will be evaluated by the federal and British Columbia governments in June of 1997, and every year thereafter. However, after the completion of five treaties, either government may require a special evaluation of the MOU 'in meeting the objective of concluding negotiations with First Nations.' Any amendments to the MOU can be undertaken only with the written consent of both governments. After June 1997, the MOU may be terminated by either government with one year's written notice, but the terms of the MOU will continue to apply to those negotiations for which an Agreement in Principle has been reached before the notice of termination is given.[14]

The First Nations Participating in the Treaty-Making Process

Many First Nations and tribal groups have entered the treaty-making process. As of the fall of 1995, a total of forty-seven aboriginal groups in British Columbia have submitted SOIs. Appendix B provides a list of the aboriginal groups who are presently involved in negotiations, and the stage of the process each group has reached.

However, as noted earlier, the treaty-making process is a voluntary one, and no First Nation is compelled to participate. Those aboriginal groups who have decided not to participate offer two main reasons. Many of the aboriginal groups in the interior of the province argue that the treaty negotiation process is illegitimate, since it involves rights to land and resources that have never been ceded by First Nations to the Canadian governments.[15] As will be recalled from Chapter 1, when the British asserted sovereignty over British Columbia, imperial policy and international law provided a variety of ways in which a sovereign nation could acquire foreign land. If the land was already occupied by indigenous people, one method was to obtain the consent of the aboriginal people to cede some or all of their land to the acquiring state. The rights and obligations of the parties would then be codified in a treaty. This was the approach used by Governor Douglas during the 1850s on Vancouver Island. To some First Nations, because they have never formally ceded their lands to any Canadian government, the negotiation of treaties is seen as premature.

A second reason for choosing not to negotiate involves a challenge to the provincial government's role. The First Nations in the interior of the province belong to the Union of British Columbia Indian Chiefs (UBCIC), and do not acknowledge as legitimate the role of the British Columbia government in the negotiations. According to the UBCIC, the treaties that are to be concluded in British Columbia should be negotiated on a nation-to-nation basis, between the First Nations and the federal government. Since British Columbia is not a nation, it should not be involved in the negotiations. While this argument is plausible on both historical and legal grounds, it appears unworkable. Treaty negotiations involve land and natural resources that fall within the legislative scope and proprietary interests of British Columbia. To argue the province should be excluded from treaty negotiations would necessitate separate negotiations between Canada and British Columbia at a later date, and could therefore extend and complicate the treaty-making process.[16]

Openness of the Treaty Negotiations

The British Columbia Claims Task Force recommended that non-aboriginal interests be represented at the negotiating table by federal and provincial governments. The initial response by the provincial government was to create a third party advisory committee. Established in 1992, the Treaty Advisory Committee (TAC) was charged with representing to the provincial government the interests of major provincial business, labour, and fish and wildlife groups during the treaty negotiations. A year later TAC was restructured and renamed the Treaty Negotiation Advisory Committee (TNAC). It would represent similar sectoral interests, but now to both federal and provincial governments. TNAC is comprised of thirty-one members, organized into five sectoral subcommittees: Governance; Fisheries; Lands and Forests; Wildlife; and Energy, Mines, and Petroleum Resources. They are charged with developing an effective consultation process as a necessary building block to support the treaty negotiations.

Yet during the latter part of 1993 and into 1994, concerns arose surrounding the breadth of third party and public involvement in the negotiations. The provincial government responded in two ways. On 19 September 1994, an agreement between the province and the Union of British Columbia Municipalities was announced, guaranteeing the participation of local governments and regional districts in the negotiations. The agreement called for:

- the identification of local government interests which may be affected by treaties
- the establishment of a consultation process with local governments in each treaty area
- the creation of local government treaty advisory committees that would have representatives at each negotiating table
- and a process whereby local government representatives could advise provincial negotiators on issues of concern to local governments.[17]

The following day, Premier Harcourt outlined the provincial government's principles for openness in the negotiations. Stating that 'public confidence in the negotiating process [was] essential for successful agreements,' Harcourt enumerated a number of ideals that provincial negotiators would take with them to the treaty talks, including:

- The negotiations would be open to observation by anyone.
- Some negotiations would be broadcast on television.
- Province-wide mandates would be set, in which the bottom line and goalposts of the negotiations would be made public.
- Information on the negotiations would be disseminated.
- All Agreements in Principle would be 'taken to the public for review, and final settlements [would be] ratified by the Legislative Assembly of British Columbia.'[18]

This commitment to openness by the provincial government and, in particular, the views of members of TNAC regarding their role in the treaty negotiations will be discussed in Chapter 4.

Interim Measures Agreements

One of the recommendations put forward by the British Columbia Claims Task Force was the creation of a series of interim measures agreements (IMAs). Forged on the basis of a government-to-government relationship between the provincial government and First Nations, IMAs are intended primarily to regulate the management and use of land and natural resources during the period preceding the conclusion of treaties, so that the interests of the parties (including potential aboriginal rights) are balanced and protected. IMAs are also used to promote cooperative and integrated land and resource management schemes, and may deal with the jurisdiction and authority of First Nations in a number of policy areas, such as education, child welfare, justice, health or taxation, or any other matter agreed upon by the parties.[19] In some ways IMAs are similar to interlocutory injunctions issued by a court, in that they are a temporary or provisional arrangement of the rights and obligations of the parties to a particular matter or over a specific issue. They do not purport to declare the rights of the parties conclusively, or to settle any aspect of the issue. IMAs were used in the treaty negotiations that preceded the land claim agreements in the Yukon and the Northwest Territories.

There are two general types of IMAs. One type is referred to as program-related interim measures. These arrangements are connected with the ongoing responsibilities of the various ministries of the provincial government, and are entered into either to fulfil the government's fiduciary duty to aboriginal people or to pursue certain policy commitments (e.g., to encourage economic growth and development). They may be forged prior to a First Nation's decision to enter into formal treaty negotiations, and in no way do they bind the parties during subsequent negotiations. The negotiation and implementation of this type of agreement is considered by the provincial government to be part of its overall responsibility as a government. Any related costs must be accommodated within the particular ministry's program budget or by funds specifically allocated in the base budget for this purpose.[20]

The second type of IMA is designated as a treaty-related interim measure. Such an arrangement is associated with treaty negotiations; it protects the integrity of agreements already reached at the negotiating table until a treaty can be signed and implemented, but does not displace or limit the scope of treaty negotiations. In addition, a treaty-related interim measure must be submitted to the provincial cabinet for approval. The cost of negotiating this type of IMA is part of the treaty-making process and, consequently, included in the negotiating budget of the provincial Ministry of Aboriginal Affairs.[21]

Some observers have looked upon IMAs favourably. A treaty-related interim measure ensures the possibility of negotiating a treaty that contains some guarantee of land and natural resources that will be necessary to sustain future generations of aboriginal people. Both types of IMAs present First Nations and Canadian governments with the opportunity to learn effective negotiating styles, to develop institutional arrangements so treaty negotiations can proceed smoothly, and to begin to establish a relationship between the parties based on mutual trust and respect.[22] However, all IMAs contain some date at which they will expire, and once this occurs, the parties decide whether to renew or replace such agreements. Their provisions can also be incorporated into subsequent treaties if all parties agree.

The provincial government has stipulated certain conditions regarding the formation of IMAs. They must be consistent with existing legislation, and they do not affect the province's final statutory authority over the management of public lands. They do not create a power of veto for First Nations over Crown decisions, and they will not define settlement boundaries before there has been substantive discussion and agreement on these matters at the negotiating tables. Moreover, program-related IMAs do not determine questions of ownership or jurisdiction in discussions of land and resource management, nor do they abrogate areas of federal legislative jurisdiction.[23]

3
The Issues to Be Negotiated

The scope of issues that will dominate the treaty negotiations is immense. Ultimately, the treaties will have a lasting effect on aboriginal communities, on the management of lands and natural resources, and on the nature of the relationship between aboriginal and non-aboriginal people in British Columbia. There is no blueprint for the treaties. The contents of each will vary. And they will reflect the unique circumstances and goals of the First Nations to whom they apply. Moreover, as the talks progress, and as the parties refine their respective negotiating positions and begin to deal with the operational requirements of the issues before them, new issues will emerge, and some may even be discarded at the bargaining table. This is part of the fluid nature of any negotiating process and should not been seen as a sign of indecision on the part of the negotiators.

The Main Issues
While most of the negotiating teams have yet to devise detailed positions, there are nevertheless some issues common to all the treaty talks, including:

- forms of self-government
- acknowledgment of lands and resources, other than Crown land, which were alienated as a result of rural and urban development and industry
- economic development initiatives for aboriginal people, including jobs in resource extraction and management
- a greater role for aboriginal people and communities in the management of fisheries, mining, and forestry.

The scope of these issues will be refined as the talks proceed. But some issues, such as the quantity of treaty settlement land, will affect other items included in treaty settlement packages. For example, in the Lower

Mainland of British Columbia, at least six treaties are expected to be concluded, affecting an aboriginal population of approximately 4,800. The issue of additional reserve land is therefore very important. Each of the First Nations (i.e., Musqueam, Squamish, Burrard, Katzie, and Tsawwassen), due in large part to population increases, desires an extension of their existing reserve land through the acquisition of unoccupied Crown land or through the purchase of private property. Yet large tracts of affordable land are rather scarce, which could leave these communities 'land poor' in relation to those aboriginal communities in less populated regions of the province. As a result, the financial component of the settlement packages in the Lower Mainland could be more heavily endowed, offering the possibility that some First Nations could purchase property adjacent to their reserves. This has been the hope of Squamish in North Vancouver, who expressed an interest in purchasing a suburban development project next to their reserve in that city.[1]

In addition, some of the First Nations located on Vancouver Island and in the Peace River District seek to alter the size of the reserve land initially set aside for them. Some of the treaties arranged by Douglas did not account for land shared between aboriginal families or tribes, nor did they account for the land that was occupied by aboriginal groups prior to 1850 and continued to be occupied. In relation to Treaty Eight, many of the aboriginal groups who signed adhesions did so with some reluctance, since they felt their traditional territory was far too immense to sell for the price offered by the federal government.

Specific Issues for Some First Nations

The Sechelt Indian Band
The Sechelt Indian Band is a Coast Salish band located on the Sechelt Peninsula, approximately 58 kilometres northwest of Vancouver. Sechelt is an aboriginal word meaning 'place of shelter from the sea.' During the mid-1990s, the population of the band was approximately 910. The band's tribal base is located at the head of Sechelt Inlet, immediately adjacent to the non-aboriginal communities in the District of Sechelt.[2]

What sets the Sechelt apart from other First Nations in the province is their relative autonomy from the federal government. The Sechelt Indian Band Self-Government Act, enacted in 1986, provides the band with control and ownership of band lands and resources, the ability to negotiate with the federal government over the payment of block grants to the band, and the legislative framework for self-government – all without abrogating or derogating from any aboriginal and treaty rights, including land claims. The band can tax both aboriginal and non-aboriginal people occupying

Sechelt lands. But other kinds of ordinary municipal taxes, such as school and hospital taxes, apply to both aboriginal and non-aboriginal people. The Sechelt Constitution gives Sechelt by-laws the status of federal laws, thereby creating a sphere of legislative authority for the Sechelt, separate from provincial laws. Moreover, a provincial statute, the Sechelt Indian Government District Enabling Act, recognizes Sechelt government juris-diction over Sechelt and non-Sechelt occupiers of the band's land. The Act allows the district to employ provincial statutes and treats the district as a municipality for receiving provincial benefits and programs.[3]

Completed in December 1994, the Sechelt band's Framework Agree-ment sets out a number of issues that may form the basis of an Agreement in Principle later in the treaty-making process. The list of issues it contains is extensive, so only a select number will be discussed here. The Sechelt expect that once a Final Agreement is achieved with both orders of gov-ernment, it will constitute a land claims agreement, subject to constitu-tional protection under section 35 of the Constitution Act of 1982.[4]

The Framework Agreement deals first with financial compensation for 'past injustices' dating to the late 1850s. Archival information assembled by Sechelt negotiators indicates that among the injustices was the denial by the provincial government of timber resources to the Sechelt people in the area of Jervis Inlet and Porpoise Bay, as well as forcible removal of some Sechelt people in the same area.[5] The Sechelt seek compensation in the amount of $60,000 per capita, to be delivered in the form of cash, pro-grams, and other benefits. The sum is borrowed from a purported federal cabinet document written in 1984, and is based ostensibly on the com-pensation arrived at in relation to previously concluded land claims in the Canadian North, such as the James Bay and Inuvialuit Final Agreements, and the Council of Yukon Indians' Agreement in Principle. It should be noted that federal treaty negotiators deny the existence of the cabinet doc-ument. The Sechelt adjusted the figure to reflect 1994 dollar values and multiplied that figure by the number of band members as of 31 December 1994. The total amount arrived at was $77,784,980. However, while the Sechelt have noted that both federal and British Columbia governments have agreed that there is no preconceived figure set aside for compensation in the treaties, the band makes it clear that 'in the event that any subse-quent land claim settlements in British Columbia result in the payment of a higher per capita package than is received by Sechelt, [the Sechelt] reserve the right to re-open [their] settlement through [provincial arbitration laws].'[6] Put simply, this position suggests that the Sechelt will not accept a per capita compensation package smaller than that received by any other British Columbia First Nation negotiating a treaty.

The Sechelt also wish to expand their current land and resource base.

This will primarily involve provincial Crown land in the areas of Narrows Inlet, Salmon Inlet, as well as some natural resources in nearby creeks. Much of this area is subject to licences of occupation. The total value of these lands will be arrived at through treaty negotiations and will be deducted from the value of the band's overall compensation package. However, the Sechelt maintain that the lands and resources purchased will be part of their aboriginal territory and must not, as of 15 February 1995, fall within the jurisdiction of the Municipality of Powell River or the District of Sechelt, unless these municipalities agree to forsake such lands and subject them to the negotiations.[7]

With regard to subsurface mineral rights, the Sechelt wish to be sole owners of the minerals which lie beneath their lands. In exchange, the band agrees to release the federal and British Columbia governments from all claims arising from the denial of aboriginal title to their territory, but will retain all their aboriginal rights as they are defined at present and in the future. Such a partial *quid pro quo* is consistent with the Sechelt's earlier bargaining position under the federal comprehensive claims process. In 1984 when their claim was first submitted, the Sechelt agreed to the extinguishment of aboriginal title to their traditional territory in exchange for self-government legislation. Furthermore, as self-government affects resource revenue-sharing, the Sechelt agreed to share with the British Columbia government, on a 50 per cent-50 per cent basis in perpetuity, the royalties and other payments derived from taking any natural resources from Sechelt or non-Sechelt lands.[8]

The Sechelt maintain that the form of self-government exercised under the Sechelt Indian Band Self-Government Act should remain in its present form. However, once treaty negotiations have been concluded, this form of governance should be constitutionally entrenched, and seen as a 'unique order of government,' existing alongside the provisions affecting Sechelt government contained in the Municipal Act of British Columbia. To maintain Sechelt-government relations, a Liaison Committee has been established, with one appointee each from the Sechelt band, the federal government, and the provincial government, so that there will be a continuous flow of communication on all matters relating to the Sechelt to all the parties involved. The first meeting took place in August of 1995.[9] All the institutions, authorities, and powers of taxation of the Sechelt will continue as they are, and the block grants to the band from the federal government will continue in their present form.[10]

The Framework Agreement affects a whole host of other issues, including: water management, parks and protected areas, environmental assessment procedures, third party interests, the management and protection of natural resources on Sechelt land, and wildlife harvesting and management. Consequently, the Sechelt hold that an entity to be known as the Sechelt Aboriginal Territory Governing Council should be established, to make decisions on these matters and to grant licences and tenures.[11]

Finally, the Sechelt submit that their members should continue to enjoy access to unoccupied provincial Crown lands in order to exercise their aboriginal rights of hunting and fishing. The Sechelt will not deny anyone access to their lands as long as they obtain the consent of the Sechelt.[12]

The Nuu'Chah'Nulth Tribal Council

Once known as the Nootka, the thirteen First Nations represented by the Nuu'Chah'Nulth Tribal Council are located on the western half of Vancouver Island. Their claim to land and resources affects much of this section of the Island, from about Port Renfrew, north to the tip of Cape Cook. Similar to many other First Nations in the province, the people represented by the Nuu'Chah'Nulth Tribal Council assert that their sovereignty has existed in this area since time immemorial, and base their claim for land and other benefits on the fact that they have never ceded, surrendered, or released their aboriginal title.[13]

As part of their initial negotiating position, the tribal council have indicated that they will recognize the rights of fee simple title holders, provided that title was granted on or prior to 22 October 1994 – the date on which their hereditary chiefs made a formal declaration to this effect. And fee simple title holders whose land is affected by the settlement of treaties will be offered compensation in an amount arrived at through negotiations between the tribal council and both orders of government.[14]

The tribal council also notes that the existing reserve base of their members should be converted to treaty settlement lands, and that the total land base ultimately agreed upon be 'sufficient to meet [their] cultural, spiritual, and community needs, including housing, recreation, infrastructure, and other uses, as well as to provide economic, recreational, and other opportunities for our members.'[15] In addition, the title to these lands should not be held in fee simple but rather 'constitutionalized' in section 35 of the Constitution Act of 1982. Like all other First Nations involved in the treaty-making process, the tribal council argues that the constitutional entrenchment of their treaty settlement lands is not only consistent with their aboriginal rights, but 'will protect [their] collective interests and ... avoid dilution of [their] resources.'[16] Doubtless, placing treaty settlement lands in the constitution will seriously affect (if not negate) federal land expropriation powers over aboriginal reserve land.

The tribal council maintains they should have full authority, control, and jurisdiction over these lands (lands to be used by First Nations' peoples exclusively), and that the kind of self-governing arrangement they seek will have powers that extend to Nuu'Chah'Nulth people in other parts of Canada. In the words of one of their position papers:

> Any rights and arrangements we negotiate will apply to all Nuu'Chah'-Nulth regardless of their residence ... We will negotiate what we believe will be unique arrangements by which our rights as Nuu'Chah'Nulth people can be provided to all our people, regardless of where they live in Canada. This negotiation may include (but will not be limited to) the establishment of treaty lands in certain urban areas. We believe that these arrangements will be unique because treaty lands established in urban areas will be accessible to and used by members of all First Nations, notwithstanding the fact that the particular urban area is within the territory of a particular First Nation. We anticipate this initiative might entail discussion and agreement with neighbouring First Nations as well as with British Columbia and Canada.[17]

With regard to fish and ocean resource management, the Nuu'Chah'Nulth wish to negotiate an arrangement with the federal government that would recognize the cross-boundary characteristic of these resources and, more specifically, one that would recognize Nuu'Chah'Nulth ownership and jurisdiction over specific fishing areas where halibut and cod stocks lie. Moreover, like the neighbouring Makah Indians in northwestern Washington State who wish to resume whale hunting, the tribal council also contend they will decide 'when and how [they] will exercise their right to hunt whales again.'[18]

The tribal council's position on provincial Crown land affected by the treaty negotiations is clear. Existing park boundaries should be subject to the talks and could be changed, since this land presently encompasses a significant portion of the traditional lands and resources of the Nuu'-Chah'Nulth people. Present and future rights-of-way will also be subject to the negotiations, as will access by non-aboriginal people to treaty settlement lands.[19]

Ultimately, the treaty sought by the Nuu'Chah'Nulth would contain provisions relating to all the issues noted above. The treaty benefits package should also include monetary compensation for the prior alienation of lands and resources, to be used for the benefit of future generations of Nuu'Chah'Nulth people. This is seen as a cornerstone of the tribal council's intention 'to create and ensure equality and economic stability for [their] Nations and communities ... [and to] establish [their] place within Canada.'[20] Furthermore, while the treaty would be entrenched in the constitution, parts of it would be susceptible to change through an amending formula involving the participation and consent of both orders of government. It would also include a dispute resolution mechanism in case any changes cannot be agreed upon by all three sides. This will allow parts of the treaty to evolve to meet new and emerging circumstances. The treaty would also contain an enforcement clause, binding the parties to all aspects of the treaty.[21]

The Gitxsan First Nation

The Gitxsan are part of the Tsimshian ethnic division, with reserve land near the towns of Hazelton and Smithers in northwestern British Columbia. They claim ownership and control over more than 11,000 square kilometres of their traditional territory, near the Upper Skeena and Bulkley Rivers. The claim is based on the Gitxsan use and occupation of the land since time immemorial. They see the settlement of the claim as the foundation on which their sovereignty can be exercised in the areas of land use, education, social and economic development, and in relations with local and regional governments. The Gitxsan have always rejected the reserve system and maintain that they have openly occupied their traditional lands as required by seasonal game activities. Since 1908 the Gitxsan have pressured the federal government to settle their claim through a variety of channels, including negotiation, the federal comprehensive claims process, and litigation.

In an agreement with the British Columbia government, the Gitxsan agreed to adjourn their appeal to the Supreme Court of Canada in the *Delgamuukw* case for a period of one year.[22] During this time they worked with federal and provincial treaty negotiators to arrive at a Framework Agreement. The Agreement was signed on 13 July 1995. Incidentally, some Gitxsan argue that the adjournment of the case was an essential precondition for the federal and provincial government's participation in treaty talks with the Gitxsan.[23] While such concessions are often a natural part of any negotiating process, it appears that not all of the First Nations who have joined the treaty-making process would agree they joined in a completely voluntarily fashion.

The Gitxsan seek to establish a treaty that rejects the paternalism of their past relationship with the federal government. Grounded in the notion of the pre-existence and continuing existence of their aboriginal rights, such a treaty will be absent of any preconditions set by the provincial and federal governments over the selection and control of lands and resources, or over the style of government to be exercised by the Gitxsan. With regard to self-government, the Gitxsan wish to have a form of governance based on their traditional systems: it will recognize the authority of hereditary chiefs[24] and will be decentralized in its decision-making capacities. A recognition of the traditional system of governance will replace the band council system imposed upon the Gitxsan through the Indian Act.

Among many First Nations in Canada, there has been a considerable amount of friction between traditional systems of government and the band council system. Among the Gitxsan as well, the band council system is seen as foreign to their political traditions, imposing colonial structures and norms of leadership and thus preventing true Native leadership from emerging to represent the interests of the people. A similar sentiment is reflected in the words of hereditary chief Don Ryan: 'The ballot box is a waste of time; what we seek is the recognition of our traditional form of governance, based on understanding and agreement among the various houses of Gitxsan, and one that was given to us by the Creator, but also developed by us over many years.'[25]

The British Columbia Court of Appeal's decision in *Delgamuukw* and the federal government's position on the scope of aboriginal self-government indicate it is to be confined largely to the internal affairs of the particular First Nation.[26] The Gitxsan see few difficulties with this view of the jurisdiction of their form of self-government. But what remains contentious, and what must be worked out in negotiations, is the manner in which Gitxsan and federal and provincial laws could work together harmoniously in policy areas of mutual concern. Indeed, any sharing of policy fields (e.g., wildlife harvesting and fisheries) becomes problematic if there are competing conceptions of the ultimate goals, such as 'conservation' and 'sustainable development.'

The desire of the Gitxsan to be an equal partner alongside Canadian governments also colours the Gitxsan view of the quality and quantity of future treaty settlement lands. Again, they seek the removal of their long-standing dependence on government. This goal is particularly germane to the federal model of land selection, which would allow the Gitxsan to choose from land parcels designated by the federal and provincial governments, with little or no aboriginal input. This model considers only the interests that have developed in the land to the present time, rather than the future interests of the Gitxsan. Consequently, it is viewed as a socially divisive continuation of the reserve system, based on the presumption of aboriginal subordination to Canadian governments. What the Gitxsan seek is a land selection model that incorporates all interests, both present and future, and that creates the stability needed to maintain capital investment.[27]

However, at the time of writing, the future of the negotiations with the Gitxsan appears to be in doubt. In January 1996, after giving notice to the Gitxsan, the province walked away from the talks. The Accord of

Recognition and Respect, signed in June 1994, which had halted the Gitxsan appeal before the Supreme Court of Canada, had expired, and the province did not wish to extend the agreement further. To the Gitxsan, this move by the province was not unexpected and seemed to be linked to the province's overall strategy in the negotiations. According to Chief Elmer Derrick: 'Even though we wanted to continue the talks, they [the provincial negotiators] told Don [Ryan] and others that no treaties would be signed during their [the provincial government's] first term.'[28] To Derrick and other Gitxsan the strategy behind the province's decision was clear: the province did not wish to be put in the politically undesirable position of having to defend treaties with aboriginal groups to the public and the opposition parties. The Agreement in Principle with the Nisga'a, signed in March 1996, would be sufficient to demonstrate to the non-aboriginal public and to other aboriginal groups that progress was being made in negotiating treaties. But it would also provoke much of the resistance to treaties voiced by affected third parties, such as the forest sector.[29] Concluding similar arrangements with other aboriginal groups would not only broaden this opposition, but it could also force the provincial government to fight an impending election solely on the issue of aboriginal treaties. It would be much more astute for the government to work out an agreement with the Gitxsan and other groups after winning a second term of office, thus giving the government at least four years of 'breathing room' to conclude and implement additional treaties.

The Gitxsan asked the British Columbia Treaty Commission to help work around this impasse in the negotiations by offering mediation and by engaging in a fact-finding process to determine the precise causes of the breakdown. The provincial government would only meet with the commission separately and not as part of a larger meeting with federal government negotiators and the Gitxsan. Consequently, three separate meetings were held in March 1996, and a report was to be released by the treaty commission later, outlining the causes of the breakdown and recommending measures to be taken by all parties to get the negotiations back on track.

Federal and Provincial Government Positions

There is a remarkable degree of consistency in the negotiating positions of the federal and British Columbia governments. Unfortunately, due to the early stages of many of the negotiations, the positions of the governments are somewhat vague, save the federal government's more recent position on aboriginal self-government. Nevertheless, the governments do offer some basic parameters for the purposes of discussion. These fall into four categories: lands and resources, natural resources, financial benefits to First Nations, and self-government.

Lands and Resources

Two kinds of land are involved in the treaty negotiations: existing reserve land and Crown lands. Native reserve land is subject to the legislative authority of the federal government, pursuant to section 91(24) of the Constitution Act of 1867. Crown lands are mainly provincially owned lands, although some of the land transferred to First Nations could be surplus federal Crown land.[30]

As noted earlier, there could be considerable differences in the amount of land available for the settlement of specific treaties. For treaties concluded with First Nations in major urban centres, the land allotment will be less than that awarded to Native groups in rural areas, due to the limited availability of urban land and its higher market value. However, there is no pre-determined amount of land designated for each First Nation in treaty talks. Instead, the following variables may be used to guide provincial negotiators in their decisions affecting land:

- the objectives of the First Nations, which in some cases may be met without negotiating land ownership
- the quality and quantity of Native reserve land presently held by the First Nation
- the availability of Crown land in the area of the specific treaty proposed, and the value of this land and its resources
- local economic opportunities available to aboriginal peoples
- the nature and scope of provincial and public interests in the area of the settlement
- the nature and extent of private interest (e.g., leases, licences) in lands and resources in the treaty settlement area
- the relationship of land to other components of the treaty, such as the balance of cash and land.[31]

The land base of existing reserves will be incorporated into the total treaty settlement packages, with the overall land held by all First Nations, once all treaties have been concluded, amounting to less than 5 per cent of the total land mass of the province. A critical assessment of this proposal by the provincial government is offered in Chapter 4.

The extent to which forms of private property may be appropriated for the purposes of treaties does not vary between governments. British Columbia maintains that the province 'will not expropriate or interfere with privately owned lands to conclude treaty.'[32] However, the federal government has suggested that any sale of land held in fee simple will be made on a voluntary basis.[33] Most First Nations have stated that they do not wish to upset the interests of private property, but those in urban areas are interested in purchasing private lands to accommodate the needs of a growing population. Thus, it is plausible that, although neither order of government wishes to appropriate private property directly, lands held in fee simple may become part of treaty settlement lands if the owners feel inclined or can be persuaded to sell their interests in the land to the governments. Moreover, since the provincial government has included non-exclusive tenures in its definition of private interests on Crown lands, based on experiences in other jurisdictions, these interests may indeed be purchased in order to clear the way for treaty settlement.[34] However, the provincial government has indicated that any 'disruption to existing interests, including interests held by individuals, corporations, or local governments, will be avoided whenever possible.'[35]

In respect of land tenure, the federal government desires a form of holding that can be used by First Nations to become self-reliant and that eradicates the paternalistic nature of the federal government's relationship with aboriginal peoples. Consequently, the discretionary powers of Ottawa under the Indian Act as they affect reserve lands will be eradicated, along with the fiduciary obligations which these powers create.[36]

It is not clear whether First Nations will operate as full-fledged sovereign entities with legislative powers that will override those of the federal and provincial governments. Many proposals put forth by First Nations in the negotiations contemplate certain policy areas in which aboriginal law will eventually be paramount over provincial law and even federal law. Both orders of government have suggested that the jurisdiction of First Nations over treaty settlement lands will be subject to federal and British Columbia laws of general application, unless specified otherwise in particular treaties. Those lands selected or retained by First Nations as part of their settlement should offer 'limited' or 'reasonable' forms of access to the public, government, and commercial interests. However, the provincial government sees highways, rights-of-way, and 'sites integral to the development of these networks' remaining within provincial jurisdiction.[37]

With regard to subsurface rights, Ottawa feels that the holders of subsurface resource entitlements will have access to treaty settlement lands where such access is necessary for 'exploration, development, and production purposes.'[38] But this right of entry will be conditional upon payment to the relevant First Nation of compensation, if it results in damage to settlement lands. This obligation is not all that peculiar, since development companies have always been required to pay remuneration to aboriginal communities if any harm occurred to their reserve lands as a result of development. Moreover, the federal government is clear that it will retain its powers of expropriation in relation to aboriginal land, but these powers will not be used in an arbitrary fashion.

Natural Resources

As part of their jurisdictional responsibility over fisheries, the federal government envisions the development of a West Coast strategy for sustainable fish harvesting by all users – aboriginal and non-aboriginal alike. But such a strategy will not preclude an annual entitlement to fish by First Nations, carried out by aboriginal management and co-management regimes, both locally and on a regional basis. Such an entitlement will presumably take the form of an extension to the Aboriginal Fisheries Strategy already in place in British Columbia. In addition, third party interests (i.e., commercial and recreational fisheries, fish processors, and non-consumptive users) will be identified and taken into account throughout the treaty negotiations. If existing fisheries are disrupted by changes to be included in treaty settlement packages, Ottawa has stated they will offer an 'equitable resolution,' where possible.[39]

The federal government supports the province in the negotiation of certain preferential and/or exclusive wildlife harvesting rights for aboriginal peoples on Crown land. This position can be viewed as a continuation of the practice in many aboriginal treaties throughout Canada of allowing Native people to maintain hunting and fishing rights on unoccupied Crown land. Presumably, the entitlement will centre on hunting and fishing for food, which have enjoyed special legal status because they were seen by the courts as occupations 'within the core of Indianness.'[40] Ottawa hopes that such rights are compatible with conservation needs and that global objectives receive consideration.[41]

The provincial government has proposed a similar right of aboriginal people to harvest trees and other flora of the forest. And aboriginal people are expected to exercise managing authority over forests on treaty settlement lands. This includes conducting environmental impact assessments of projects to be undertaken on these lands, and engaging in environmental protection measures, as long as methods and practices are consistent with those used by the federal and British Columbia governments. The regulatory and decision-making powers of the aboriginal managing authorities will, however, be required to consult third party interests, the public, and government, if particular issues of concern arise.[42]

Financial Benefits

The cost-sharing agreement between the federal and British Columbia governments addresses most of the positions of either government in relation to financial benefits to First Nations as part of treaty settlements. The financial components of treaties will comprise cash payments and other benefits, which will be seen as cash equivalents. In negotiating the cash component of a treaty, the federal government will consider the overall cost of reaching a settlement, as well as the costs associated with acquiring third party interests. Payments made to First Nations will be indexed over a designated period of years, in amounts that will permit effective management by aboriginal groups. However, all financial benefits will be applied first to loans incurred by First Nations to support their negotiations in the treaty talks. The cash component of settlements will be considered by the federal government as capital transfer and thus exempt from taxation. Nevertheless, any income derived from the cash component will be subject to the provisions of the federal Income Tax Act.[43] Federal Crown lands will be included as cash equivalent benefits. Other cash benefits may include certain economic development initiatives for aboriginal people, or funds to be used by First Nations for specific economic activities.

Self-Government
Chapter 1 included a discussion of aboriginal self-government. Aboriginal self-government was characterized generally as the ability of aboriginal groups, through various institutional structures, to manage their own affairs according to their own priorities. Self-government was also seen as an inherent right by aboriginal people, bestowed upon them by the Creator, and not altered by the imposition of the band council system of governance laid down in the Indian Act. Chapter 1 also noted that there are varied views within aboriginal communities as to the precise mixture of powers self-governing arrangements should involve, and that each arrangement should be tailored to meet the needs of the particular Native community to which it applies.

As the treaty negotiations commenced, both federal and provincial governments laid down some vague guidelines for negotiating and implementing self-governing arrangements with First Nations, under the auspices of the British Columbia Treaty Commission. For example, while the federal government saw aboriginal self-government as an inherent right, protected by section 35(1) of the Constitution Act of 1982, specific items that would enjoy constitutional protection were described as 'those to which future generations and governments would be most appropriately bound, rather than matters of a technical, administrative or temporary nature.'[44]

In early August of 1995, the federal government released a much more specific negotiating position on the kind of self-governing arrangements it would be prepared to support. In short, self-government would resemble a municipal government, holding powers weaker than those of provincial governments. It would apply to aboriginal people on and off reserves, be subject to constitutional protection only if that was desired by the relevant First Nation, and represent a clear departure from the 'third order of government,' codified in the provisions of the 1992 Charlottetown Accord. The federal government sought to avoid 'revisiting the constitution' and to negotiate self-governing arrangements with specific First Nations rather than entertain the views of large aboriginal organizations such as the Assembly of First Nations, which dominated self-government discourse in previous years.[45]

There are some specific issues that Ottawa will not subject to the negotiations for self-government. The provisions of the Criminal Code will continue to apply to aboriginal people; and aboriginal communities will play no measurable role in the formation of international treaties, nor in the development of federal policies affecting broadcasting, banking, or national defence and security. Moreover, the entire body of the Charter of Rights and Freedoms will continue to apply to aboriginal governments and their citizens, despite Ottawa's early suggestion that the Charter's application would be confined to the 'principles of equality.'[46] Consequently, aboriginal governments will not become sovereign entities in any real sense: both federal and provincial laws will apply to First Nations, unless otherwise provided in the treaties; the federal government will retain its legislative powers to maintain 'peace, order, and good government in Canada'; and all arrangements will be conducted on the presumption of the predominance of the Canadian constitution and the federal form of government in Canada. What powers the federal government appears prepared to assign to aboriginal communities would be those law-making powers seen as internal to aboriginal communities (e.g., social services, membership in the aboriginal community, adoption and child welfare); integral to their cultures, traditions, institutions, and languages; and related to the management of their lands and natural resources.[47]

There are other powers aboriginal governments could hold, but Ottawa maintains that the incorporation of these policy areas into self-governing arrangements will be subject to negotiations with the provincial governments. Such policy areas include labour and training, the administration of justice, and environmental protection powers, to name a few. In addition, Ottawa holds that aboriginal governments of the future must be accountable to their constituents, both politically and financially, and that any funds received by First Nations from the federal government for the purposes of aboriginal governments will require a similar kind of accountability to Parliament.[48]

4
The Treaty-Making Process Considered

Despite the relative infancy of many of the treaty negotiations, the process itself has come under a significant degree of scrutiny by both aboriginal and non-aboriginal groups alike. Unfortunately, criticism of the process is all too often conflated with specific concerns over public policy on aboriginal people. However, underlying the opposition to the process is the fact that treaty-making requires a significant measure of public trust in the actions of government and First Nation negotiators. This is problematic when public support for the institutions of government has waned in recent years, and when the policies of the provincial government in Victoria came under increasing opposition as the term of its first mandate came to a close. To be sure, if the treaty-making process is to be successful, and if it is to be seen as legitimate in the eyes of the electorate, it will require the support of British Columbians.

Third Party Representation and Secrecy Surrounding the Negotiations

The British Columbia Claims Task Force recommended that non-aboriginal interests should be represented at the negotiating table by the federal and British Columbia governments. The task force found no need for a more substantive role for such interests, since it was seen as 'impractical' and as an impediment to the progress of the negotiations. Consequently, the task force directed the governments 'to consider special procedural arrangements to involve non-aboriginal interests during the negotiations,'[1] particularly during the development of Framework Agreements.

The British Columbia government responded to this directive by creating an advisory committee for major third party interests, known as the Treaty Advisory Committee (TAC). It was responsible for representing the interests of major provincial business, labour, and fish and wildlife groups to the provincial government during the talks. The following year TAC was modified somewhat and named the Treaty Negotiation Advisory Committee (TNAC). This body was still composed of major third party interests, but now its interests would be represented by both orders of government during the negotiations.

However, during the early stages of the process, when most First Nations had only filed a Statement of Intent (SOI) with the commission, problems arose concerning the role of TNAC. In a 1994 letter[2] to both Indian Affairs Minister Ron Irwin and Aboriginal Affairs Minister John Cashore, members of TNAC presented a series of concerns, grouped into four categories:

(1) Confidentiality: Members of TNAC argued that the rules of confidentiality to which they were bound were too sweeping and placed a severe constraint on their ability to communicate with and to obtain information and policy guidance from those they represent.

(2) Interim Measures Agreements: TNAC members indicated displeasure that they had not been consulted adequately and involved in the development of pre-treaty co-management and other interim measures agreements. This was seen as contrary to their understanding that governments would seek advice and input from TNAC prior to concluding such agreements.

(3) Minutes and Accountability: There was also a concern about the general lack of consistent written records of TNAC committee meetings. Most meetings simply listed those in attendance and provided written summaries of the presentations given by the governments' representatives. Indeed, there was no consistent record of the questions raised and comments offered by TNAC members, nor of any actions that might be taken by the governments in response to the issues raised.

(4) Public Education and Information: The final problem centred around the desire by TNAC to have a more formal role in the public education and information efforts already being undertaken by the governments and by the First Nations.

The letter was made public by the Vancouver media.[3] Within a week both governments declared their support for a more open treaty-making process. For their part, Ottawa laid down a series of 'considerations' which would guide their commitment to this goal. Henceforth, members of TNAC would work directly with and have access to the federal departments involved in the negotiations, and be able to provide comments on the various options being developed for discussion at the negotiating tables. Any Agreements in Principle forged between the governments and First Nations would be explained to the public and discussed prior to ratification. There was also a commitment to a greater exchange of information. However, Ottawa made it clear that it would not release to the public the precise mandates of its treaty negotiators, since this would 'limit the opportunities to explore creative options, and present the other parties with the appearance of an inflexible ... situation.'[4]

Victoria sought to open up the negotiations by including local governments. In a Memorandum of Understanding between the provincial government and the Union of British Columbia Municipalities, the provincial government outlined certain issues on which local governments would be consulted, and it gave municipalities status during the negotiations and during the formulation of Framework Agreements on issues that directly affected municipalities. Local governments would then establish regional advisory committees and allow representatives of those committees to sit in on the negotiations. The representatives in each region would report back to the larger committee.[5]

However, these efforts at opening up the negotiations produced a series of related problems. For example, many local politicians and their officials found they were unfamiliar with the range of issues before them – a problem made worse by having little prior knowledge of the topics that would be placed on the negotiating table. When certain First Nations, after signing interim measures agreements, declared in public that they now had jurisdiction over large portions of the lands affected, local politicians also began to wonder whether their role in the negotiations had any real impact on the actions of the provincial government.[6] These doubts extended to the federal government as well, after suggestions that Ottawa had its own agenda, which included approving Indian band by-laws and giving aboriginal groups new powers of taxation, without first seeking the views of municipalities.[7]

A number of First Nations and tribal groups did their part to make the negotiations more open to the public and other affected interests. In late 1994 the Sechelt Indian Band signed an 'openness agreement' whereby members of the public would be allowed to attend the band's treaty discussions. Seats around the negotiating table were reserved for both the public and the media, and a local television station positioned several cameras around the room.[8] Subsequently, the Nuu'Chah'Nulth Tribal Council signed an agreement similar to the Sechelt's, in which decisions made during the negotiations would be recorded and distributed to libraries, computer bulletin boards, and other media to ensure widespread dissemination of information. In addition, media coverage of the talks would be allowed, and the public would be notified in advance of forthcoming sessions in their region. Public attendance would be restricted only when there was a lack of space or when such attendance would harm the progress of the talks or prejudice the positions or strategies of the parties.[9]

However, such efforts seemed to do little to alleviate the concerns expressed by some members of TNAC. According to them, the provincial government continued, despite TNAC's opposition, to lay the foundation for interim measures agreements with aboriginal groups on an ad hoc basis, without any meaningful input from or reference to the affected parties. Indeed, shortly after Victoria articulated a new policy on the conclusion of such agreements (one that would involve briefing local governments and affected parties once negotiations began and offering them a chance to review the agreement), the provincial government proposed several program-related interim measures agreements with little reference to the stakeholders. One agreement gave the Gitxsan significant powers over major decisions affecting a forested area near Hazelton. Another agreement involved several First Nations in the Okanagan area, recognizing their responsibility to serve in perpetuity as protectors of the land, waters, and resources of their traditional territories south of Penticton.[10]

It must be emphasized that both of these interim measures agreements are program-related (as opposed to treaty-related). Such agreements are arranged to fulfil the government's fiduciary duty to aboriginal peoples or to pursue certain policy commitments. In no way do they bind the parties during subsequent treaty negotiations. In fact, as is the case in the agreement with the First Nations in the Okanagan area, program-related interim measures agreements can be arranged with First Nations who have decided not to enter the treaty-making process.

Nevertheless, members of TNAC continued to see their overall role in the negotiations as marginal, and made even more so by what they perceived as the inability of government negotiators to offer any satisfying explanation of the bases on which the treaty talks rested. One member of TNAC characterized their role in the following manner: 'TNAC is used by government as a means of reassuring the public. With the odd exception, TNAC finds out things after the fact. While confidentiality has disappeared, and while TNAC meetings are open, the process is simple: bureaucrats report; we listen. Our advice is ignored.'[11] A similar sentiment was expressed by the Council of Forest Industries (COFI) in respect to the province's overall approach to the treaty negotiations:

We are ... experiencing difficulty with government's approach to 'third party consultation' whereby provincial negotiators and aboriginal groups work together for weeks or months until an agreement is fully accepted by both parties before any consultation occurs. When an opportunity for third party discussion is provided, it is often under a very tight time limit. This puts 'third parties' in the awkward position of being seen as the villain in the process if changes are requested and has the effect of severely marginalizing 'third party consultation.'[12]

Others in TNAC argued that the governments have yet to offer them any legal or philosophical explanation of aboriginal rights or of the inherent right to self-government. This paucity of information led the British Columbia Chamber of Commerce to develop a series of policies on aboriginal affairs, one of which advised ministers 'to ensure their negotiators are fully cognizant of all the issues and concerns of TNAC ... if [they] are to properly represent the "third party" people of the province.'[13]

While members of TNAC have been less than satisfied with their role in the negotiations, it should be emphasized that their involvement should become more tangible – as will that of other third party interests – once the negotiations reach the Framework Agreement stage and beyond. However, if the role of third parties continues to be marginal at this stage, then the process will certainly run into problems of legitimacy. Indeed, as long as TNAC and the public are consigned to a role which is more procedural than substantive, the real substance of the treaty talks will be shrouded in secrecy. To be sure, treaty negotiations are largely dominated by governments and designed to cater to the interests of governments. And possibly both Ottawa and Victoria have learned, from the fate of the constitutional amendments in the Meech Lake and Charlottetown Accords, the extent to which the destiny of such sweeping policy changes can be scuttled once the public and interested parties obtain a meaningful and determinative voice. Nevertheless, repetition on this point is warranted: if the treaty negotiation process is to survive and if it is to receive the support of those outside the realm of government, it should be altered to incorporate third party interests more effectively. As Chuck Connaghan, former chief commissioner of the British Columbia Treaty Commission, noted: 'I think the public is right: the old model has to be re-thought. And it is possible to develop an approach that is satisfying.'[14]

This perspective is held not only by non-aboriginal people. Most of the chiefs of the First Nations involved in the negotiations agree the public must be given a more meaningful voice if the process is to succeed. However, what concerns aboriginal leaders most is the possibility that the process may be changed in such a way that it can be fouled later by any party who has a bias against the conclusion of aboriginal treaties generally. Consequently, any changes to the process must be made with the consent and participation of the First Nations involved. It would be counterproductive and indeed undermine the credibility of the treaty-making process to inject into the negotiations a more substantive element of public consultation without accommodating the concerns of aboriginal groups.

The Costs of Treaty-Making

There has been a considerable amount of attention devoted to the costs of concluding treaties. This issue can be considered best by isolating the views of two groups: those who believe the costs of negotiating treaties are too high and should be reduced significantly; and those who feel the costs of not concluding treaties will be higher in the long run because potential investment will be diverted to jurisdictions where there is no dispute over aboriginal title.

Those holding the former view have put forward a wide range of figures in support of their position. Often they cite what Native claims in Canada have cost the public already. For example, one report stated that Canadian taxpayers currently owe about $8 billion in unsettled aboriginal claims, and are 'on the hook' for 'billions more' in the years to come.[15] These figures do not represent actual liabilities, but rather 'contingent debts,' that is, amounts that may be owed to aboriginal groups, pending the outcome of litigation or negotiated settlements. A significant portion of these potential debts are related to specific claims against the Crown for alleged violations of existing treaty provisions, or other statutory obligations to aboriginal people by the Crown.

But these figures do not account for the costs of concluding treaties in British Columbia. And until August of 1995, both governments had not offered any precise figure. For example, Aboriginal Affairs Minister John Cashore stated that to reveal such costs would be unhelpful, ostensibly because to do so would compromise the province's negotiating position and place the treaty negotiations under even more public scrutiny.[16] Nevertheless, some estimates had placed the total costs of completing treaties at approximately $15 billion.[17] But in August of 1995, the media reported that $30.6 million dollars had been spent already on the negotiations, which did not include $15 million in federal loans Ottawa had made to various First Nations for their participation in the talks.[18] The $30 million was divided along the following lines: $280,000 in relocation costs for federal officials; $1.5 million to develop the province's policy on treaty negotiations; and over $1 million on travel expenses, computer equipment, and office supplies. These costs did not account for the costs of self-governing arrangements to be created in the future, nor those related to specific aboriginal economic development initiatives. Also not included were the costs of lost potential revenue as a consequence of the transfer of federal and provincial Crown land to First Nations, which could include the revenue that might be derived from timber and subsurface mineral development.

The arguments put forward by those who favour treaty settlements suggest that the costs of not settling would be higher over the long run, as the province would run the risk of losing potential investment capital and other economic development opportunities. The document which received the most attention from those who hold this view was a study conducted in 1989 by the accounting firm Price Waterhouse. The firm concluded that the price tag for not concluding treaties would be almost $1 billion in lost investment in the mining and forestry sectors alone. A further $50 million would be lost in capital expenditures annually, with an additional $75 million being delayed for approximately three years. Three hundred new jobs would not be created, and about 1,500 permanent jobs would be negatively impacted.[19]

Estimates of the cost of not settling treaties also have to consider the financial and economic benefits that may accrue to British Columbians, aboriginal people, and the governments of Canada and British Columbia from the conclusion of treaties. In a report commissioned by the British Columbia government, the accounting firm Peat Marwick (KPMG) provided a series of treaty-related outcomes, arrived at by extrapolating from the experiences of land claims in Northern Canada and from the financial arrangements set forth in the cost-sharing agreement between Canada and British Columbia.[20] While confident in the reasonableness of its estimates, KPMG was nonetheless careful to note that its predictions could be affected by a series of variables, including the negotiating positions and issues of the parties, the prevailing economic conditions at the time of settlement, and the actions of First Nations after the conclusion of treaties.[21]

The report suggested that one of the benefits that is likely to flow to British Columbians from treaty settlements is a measure of certainty in the province's investment climate. The clarification of aboriginal rights to ownership of land and natural resources would reduce the rationale for blockades, demonstrations, and other disruptions by Native groups. The treaties could also have spin-off effects for British Columbians:

> As cash payments are received by First Nations, local consumption will increase with some of this spending flowing to local businesses. Non-aboriginals are expected to benefit from the portion of this consumption that occurs outside the aboriginal community. The magnitude of the impact will depend, largely, on First Nations investment decisions. For example, successful investments in aboriginal business ventures will have a greater positive effect than passive settlements in non-domestic markets.[22]

The benefits of treaties for aboriginal people could be tremendous. Along with increases in overall employment and the greater sense of self-reliance that employment produces, the cash and its equivalents (e.g., urban land), and the resource revenues (e.g., forestry, mining, and other land-based incomes) that will flow from treaties could lead to significant increases in economic activity within aboriginal communities. The eventual participation of aboriginal governments in federal and provincial tax systems over treaty settlement land could also augment an aboriginal community's revenue base.[23]

The power of aboriginal governments to levy and collect taxes on their treaty settlement land and to provide additional public services to their citizens could be advantageous for both orders of non-aboriginal government through a reduction in existing levels of program funding. In addition, increases in aboriginal employment rates could lessen the demand for government social programs designed for aboriginal people, and for welfare and unemployment payments. Granted, the federal government administers most of these programs. But because the provincial government presently tops up many of these programs, a sizable savings could be realized. In 1994 for example, the province's total expenditures for federal programs targeted for aboriginal people amounted to $85 million.[24]

Due to the wide range of variables that could affect the negotiations and the treaty settlements, the report offered the provincial government a number of prescriptions for minimizing the uncertainty surrounding treaties while maximizing their positive impacts. Most significantly, it recommended that the provincial government develop clear mandates and controls on all financial commitments relating to treaty settlements, to avoid exceeding its financial targets. The provincial government should also encourage aboriginal groups to invest in education and training that would better equip them to make investment and resource management decisions. This preparation would allow aboriginal people to participate more effectively in new businesses and institutions with other British Columbians in the post-treaty era.[25]

The potential benefits of treaty settlements were underscored by an additional study commissioned by the federal and provincial governments. Conducted by the ARA Consulting Group, this study sought to assess the overall impact of treaties in the province, based on the experiences of land claims settlements in Canada, the United States, Australia, and New Zealand. While lacking specificity, the study found nonetheless that 'in no case [had] the resolution of land claims brought about political or economic chaos.'[26] During the post-treaty era, non-aboriginal business leaders took advantage of new opportunities, often by forming joint ventures with aboriginal groups; all of the modern treaties 'respected the accepted private land holdings and leases';[27] and the 'most important reality of the post settlement period [was] that life, generally, [had] proceeded much as before.'[28]

The study concluded by emphasizing implicitly not only the gains of having the public involved in the treaty negotiations but also the need for a reciprocal measure of understanding between aboriginal and non-aboriginal people throughout the negotiations: The best land claim agreements were 'those that [became] compacts between peoples and more than agreements between leaders and political institutions.'[29]

In addition to the potential economic and financial benefits of treaties, proponents of such arrangements inject a measure of moralism into their position, noting the costs of maintaining the status quo to aboriginal and non-aboriginal people alike. This view was put forward forcefully by Nisga'a Tribal Council president Joseph Gosnell:

> The highest cost of all which our opponents fail to factor into the hard math of land claims is the costs to taxpayers of keeping the current system. No one, not us, not non-natives, approves of the billions of dollars spent annually to keep aboriginal people in the binding poverty of our tiny reserves, beggars on our own land, sharing no part of its resource wealth.[30]

Much of the public's concern over the ultimate cost of treaty settlements is based on the costs of the Nisga'a Agreement in Principle (AIP), signed in March of 1996 by representatives of the Nisga'a Tribal Council and the British Columbia and federal governments.[31] Once the AIP is ratified by the parties, they will move toward negotiating a Final Agreement. The Final Agreement will be legally binding and constitute a treaty under section 25 and 35 of the Constitution Act of 1982.[32]

The AIP covers a wide range of items, including provisions affecting lands and resources, self-government, fisheries, financial compensation, and taxation. To illustrate, Nisga'a lands – the core treaty settlement area – will encompass approximately 1,930 square kilometres of land, to be owned communally by the Nisga'a nation, with title vested in the Nisga'a government. This land has been valued at approximately $100 million.[33] Nisga'a lands will also include 56 reserves located outside this core settlement area. Once the AIP has been ratified, these reserves will no longer be considered reserve land under the Indian Act but rather part of Nisga'a lands.[34] The Nisga'a government will own subsurface and surface resources on these lands.[35] Wood lot licences and agricultural leases on Crown land within this territory will not be Nisga'a lands but be retained by British Columbia. The Nisga'a government will control timber harvesting and management on Nisga'a lands. And the provincial government has agreed in principle to the acquisition by the Nisga'a of 150,000 cubic metres of timber forest licence outside Nisga'a lands.[36]

The primary governmental institutions of the Nisga'a nation will be the

Nisga'a Central Government and a series of Nisga'a village governments. The former will be responsible for relations between the Nisga'a nation and the British Columbia and Canadian governments. The Nisga'a constitution will set out the duties, composition, and membership of the central and village governments, and provide a role for Nisga'a elders in the interpretation of the constitution.[37] The constitution will come into force once it has been approved by at least 70 per cent of those voting in a referendum, and can be amended only with the approval of at least 70 per cent of those voting in a referendum for that purpose.[38] Non-Nisga'a citizens residing on Nisga'a lands will be consulted by the Nisga'a government over decisions it makes which 'directly and significantly' affect them, and be able to participate in and vote for subordinate elected bodies whose activities directly affect them.[39] The Nisga'a government may also appoint non-Nisga'a people to various government institutions.[40]

In terms of its legislative and administrative powers, the Nisga'a government will hold jurisdiction over a wide range of areas, including: culture, language, employment, public works, land use, and marriage. It will also continue to provide health, child welfare, and education services.[41] Subject to the approval of the British Columbia government, the Nisga'a will have their own police force and court to enforce and rule on Nisga'a laws on Nisga'a lands.[42] The rulings of the Nisga'a court can be appealed through the provincial appellate court system. The Charter of Rights and Freedoms will apply to the Nisga'a government and its institutions.[43]

As it affects fisheries, the AIP indicates that the Nisga'a will, through an agreement with the Canadian and British Columbia governments, receive a harvest allocation of 13 per cent of the total allowable catch of sockeye salmon and 15 per cent of the total allowable catch of pink salmon, for a term of 25 years.[44] This agreement will not be a land claim agreement and will not create any treaty rights under the Constitution Act of 1982.[45] Yet non-salmon species, which are used by the Nisga'a for domestic purposes, will be considered a treaty entitlement.[46] Moreover, the federal Department of Fisheries and Oceans will retain overall responsibility for conservation and fisheries management.[47] And the Nisga'a will receive $11.5 million from the federal government to purchase fishing vessels and licences so they can participate in the West Coast commercial fishery.[48]

The Nisga'a Central Government will receive from both orders of government a capital transfer of $190 million to be paid out over a number of years,[49] along with other fiscal transfers to assist in the delivery of public services and programs to both Nisga'a and non-Nisga'a citizens at levels comparable to those in northwest British Columbia.[50]

The taxation provisions of the AIP are numerous. Yet it should be noted that the Nisga'a Central Government will be tax exempt and be able to impose forms of direct taxation over Nisga'a citizens residing on Nisga'a lands for the purposes of the Nisga'a government.[51] Prior to the Final Agreement, the parties will attempt to reach an agreement on a definition and list of tax exemptions, which will include: Nisga'a government public works, Nisga'a citizens' residences, and forest resources.[52]

It should be noted that the negotiations leading to the Nisga'a AIP were not conducted under the current treaty-making process in British Columbia. Instead, they were activated by the federal government and undertaken through the federal comprehensive claims process, largely as a consequence of the Supreme Court of Canada's ruling in *Calder*. Victoria's presence in these negotiations was minimal, since until 1992 the province had refused to acknowledge aboriginal title in British Columbia. Nevertheless, the Nisga'a AIP remains significant because it has been referred to as the 'benchmark' against which all subsequent treaties with First Nations will be gauged. Indeed, when the costs of the Nisga'a AIP are extrapolated and applied to each of the First Nations presently engaged in treaty negotiations, even though the costs will be spread over a period of twenty to thirty years, they are sizable in the eyes of most non-aboriginal people. It was presumably with an awareness of this context that the provincial government announced a limit on the amount of cash and provincial Crown land that will be offered to aboriginal groups in future treaty settlements.[53]

Are Governments Offering More than Is Necessary?

In addition to concerns about secrecy and the total cost of concluding treaties, the most forceful attack on the treaty process involves the governments' mandate to negotiate treaties beyond the substance of the British Columbia Court of Appeal's ruling in *Delgamuukw*. This criticism was put forth by Melvin Smith in a 1995 book entitled *Our Home or Native Land?*

Smith's argument is relatively straightforward. The Court of Appeal decided in *Delgamuukw* that aboriginal rights are not proprietary rights at all. The current land claims process under way both at the federal level and in British Columbia, in which ownership to vast areas of land is being conveyed to the Natives, is therefore without legal support. For Smith, the judgment 'knocks away the props from much of the aboriginal agenda being pursued by the Native leadership with such acquiescence on the part of the politicians now in power both federally and provincially.'[54] The Court of Appeal's decision is the 'law of the land,' and it is 'the law on the nature of aboriginal interests on land in British Columbia.'

Some aspects of the Court's decision were covered in Chapter 1, but what does Smith suggest the Court ruled in *Delgamuukw* to support his contention? Smith cites the Court's majority decision only and categorizes portions of it under the following headings:

Ownership of the Land Claimed by the Gitxsan and Wet'suwet'en Nations. Smith argues that the Court of Appeal supported the finding of the British Columbia Supreme Court (the trial court which first heard the case) that the Gitxsan and Wet'suwet'en had not established a claim to ownership over the 22,000 square miles (35,420 square kilometres) of their traditional tribal territory. The only claim to ownership that could be sustained involved the land included in their present-day reserves.[55]

Self-Government. The Court of Appeal, finds Smith, also supported the trial judge's decision that the Gitxsan and Wet'suwet'en people held no claim to jurisdiction and no right to pass their own laws over the territory claimed, to the extent that such laws would conflict or abrogate existing federal and provincial laws over the same territory. Smith cites the Court of Appeal's reading of the distribution of legislative powers in Canada under sections 91 and 92 of the Constitution Act of 1867. These powers were deemed exhaustive of legislative power in Canada, thus leaving no room for a third order of government to be occupied by First Nations governments. For Smith, this finding struck a 'death knell to the much touted concept of the inherent right to native self-government.'[56]

Existing Aboriginal Rights and Extinguishing Aboriginal Rights. Smith noted that the Court's majority view on the nature and content of aboriginal rights was ascertained by asking what practices or activities the ancestors of aboriginal people considered to be an integral part of their distinctive culture at the time Britain asserted its sovereignty in 1846. Accordingly, aboriginal rights were characterized as the aboriginal community's 'right' to engage in those activities, associated with the use of the land they occupied, that were traditional, integral, and distinctive to their society and way of life in 1846.[57] In addition, the Court found the nature of those rights possessed by a particular aboriginal community were 'fact and site specific and could only be determined by an understanding of the history of that community, the location of its traditional territories, and the type of activity pursued within those territories, prior to European contact.'[58] Those practices which arose as a consequence of European contact did not qualify for protection as aboriginal rights. Smith cites here such activities as commercial trapping, fishing, forestry, and 'presumably most mining except for surface mining of shale, argillite and other stone integral to the aboriginal society.'[59]

As regards extinguishing aboriginal rights, Smith offers a rather cursory overview of the Court's ruling on this matter, concluding that limited aboriginal rights continued to exist in British Columbia and were not extinguished when the colony of British Columbia entered the Canadian federation in 1871.[60]

Smith's reading of the Court's majority decisions as they affected the

questions of land ownership, self-government, and the nature of aboriginal rights is correct. However, he fails to reveal all of the majority opinion
in respect of those aboriginal rights not extinguished in 1871. Two points
are significant to note. First, the Court did not rule that the Gitxsan and
Wet'suwet'en held no aboriginal title to the land areas claimed. Rather, the
majority held that because of the nature of the pleadings, this issue was
not before the Court. Consequently, while the Gitxsan and Wet'suwet'en
did not hold fee simple ownership in the land they claimed, they still had
aboriginal rights in this area, which were less than aboriginal title. Thus,
the immediate question of aboriginal title was left unaddressed by the
Court. Second, the Court ruled that Gitxsan and Wet'suwet'en people have
'unextinguished, non-exclusive aboriginal rights' that are protected by the
common law and which are now protected as existing aboriginal rights
under section 35(1) of the Constitution Act of 1982.[61] While not proprietary rights to traditional territory, such rights are nevertheless *sui generis*
rights (or rights of a 'special nature') to such land, and were considered
integral to 'a distinctive culture of an aboriginal society in existence at the
date of the assertion of [British] sovereignty.' To be sure, their characteristics may vary, depending both on the specific context in which they exist,
as well as in relation to specific fact situations.[62]

Unfortunately, the facts and submissions of the case were not specific so
as to permit the Court to offer a detailed analysis, in the appeal before
them, of whether an infringement of these rights had occurred. Nevertheless, while the Court did note that 'two or more interests can co-exist in
land less than fee simple' (e.g., a right of way for power lines and an aboriginal right to hunt over Crown land),[63] perhaps more importantly, it held
that it would not impede any attempts by aboriginal groups and Canadian
governments 'to negotiate the precise location, scope, content, and consequences of the aboriginal rights,' within the traditional territory of the
Gitxsan and Wet'suwet'en people.[64]

Such examples of cases where aboriginal rights could co-exist with other
rights over Crown land and the Court's emphasis on a negotiated settlement as to the location, scope, content, and consequences of aboriginal
rights seem to be consistent with negotiating positions taken by Ottawa
and Victoria in current treaty talks. Two examples will suffice. With regard
to treaty settlement land, as noted in Chapter 3 the federal government
seeks a form of aboriginal land holding that allows First Nations to realize
various 'community goals.' However, the land may be subject to federal
and provincial laws of general application which allow rights of access to
non-aboriginal interests. With regard to wildlife preservation areas, while
both governments are prepared to negotiate with First Nations over certain
preferential or exclusive wildlife harvesting rights, the federal government

has made it clear that such rights must be compatible with the needs of conservation. Note that in these examples no land held in fee simple is involved.

Even if one accepts Smith's view that the aboriginal policy of both orders of government and indeed their positions in the treaty negotiations go beyond the findings of entitlement by the courts, his argument assumes governments should act in certain policy areas only with the explicit approval of the courts. This assumption is wrong, and it ignores what the Court of Appeal said in *Delgamuukw*. In making policy, governments have often gone beyond what the courts have found to be legal. In so doing, they are not infringing the rule of law, nor are they, as Smith put it, inviting 'settlement based on avarice, arbitrariness, partiality, and political expediency.'[65] Rather, they are simply doing what the act of governance requires. There is no infringement of the rule of law by government as long as what is done is not illegal. And there are often specific policy reasons, such as equity and fairness, for a government to offer to a segment of the population more than what the courts have found, or would likely find, to be legal entitlements. If the public objects to what a government has done in a specific policy field, then they are entitled to register their dissatisfaction through various channels of democratic protest. To be sure, governments must act justly. But they are not bound to act, as Smith's views suggest they should, solely within the confines of the minimal requirements of a current and not yet final interpretation of the law.

The 5 Per Cent Limit on Negotiated Land and Demands for Blanket Extinguishment of Aboriginal Rights

As noted earlier in this chapter, once the provincial government became more sensitive to the kind of public scrutiny the treaty negotiations faced, and after the Vancouver media published a report which suggested the various First Nations participating in the treaty talks had claimed approximately 111 per cent of the province as their future treaty settlement land, Premier Harcourt announced that all treaty settlement lands (which include existing reserve land) would amount to approximately 5 per cent of the province.

The Council of Forest Industries (COFI) addressed this new policy in a written response questioning the province's overall position in the treaty talks. On the question of setting aside 5 per cent of the province for treaty settlement land, COFI asked first whether there was broad public support for such land transfers to First Nations and whether such opportunities to increase land holdings should be extended similarly to non-aboriginal persons and entities.[66] COFI further questioned the equity of such assignments indirectly, by asking whether there was support among British

Columbians for the notion of an aboriginal population of 3 per cent holding some form of title to 5 per cent of British Columbia, while the remaining 97 per cent of the non-aboriginal population held fee simple title to only about 6 per cent of the province's land.[67]

Doubtless, offering some answers to these questions is a task the provincial government should undertake. But from an aboriginal perspective, the 5 per cent formula raises some equally important questions. For example, as regards the quality of future treaty settlement land, it is not clear whether aboriginal and non-aboriginal people will be involved in the selection process. In Chapter 3 it was noted that the Gitxsan were displeased with the province's 'land selection model,' whereby provincial negotiators indicate to First Nations which parcels of land would be available as possible treaty settlement land. If such lands hold little commercial potential (the Gitxsan, for example, have made it clear the land offered to them in their negotiations is not the land they wish to have included in their treaty), one is left to question the ultimate viability of any land use initiatives contained in future treaties, which are designed to foster aboriginal economic development. And if any such treaty settlement land is of limited commercial value, then can the land selection model be seen as a continuation of the reserve system in British Columbia – a system that has been characterized by little aboriginal participation and consent?

COFI made it clear that if transfers of Crown land do occur, then a '*quid pro quo* (i.e., something for something) was in order.'[68] For them, part of the 'aboriginal *quid pro quo*' would require the removal of the burden of aboriginal rights from lands remaining as Crown lands once treaties were concluded. This would see aboriginal people exchange 'intangible, common law rights, with limited economic value'[69] for concrete assets such as lands, jurisdiction, and public assets, defined in a treaty, which could contribute to the self-sufficiency of aboriginal communities. On remaining Crown lands (i.e., those outside treaty settlement lands), aboriginal people should have the same rights as all other Canadians. Consequently, aboriginal people using Crown land for hunting and fishing would follow the same regulations as all other British Columbians, buying the same licences and participating in the same public land management processes. Among other potential benefits, this approach would give Crown land managers the ability 'to achieve the level of consistency, dependability, and certainty that is required by the many commercial and recreational licensees on Crown land.'[70]

COFI's proposal (which is a call for the blanket extinguishment of aboriginal title) holds a certain philosophical appeal for most non-aboriginal people, primarily because it is consistent with a certain kind of liberal ideology that holds supreme the notion of individual equality and discounts singling out a segment of the population for certain entitlements based on aboriginal ancestry. One also suspects that it is influenced by the rather negative public view of other government initiatives for aboriginal people, such as fisheries strategies, which have come under scrutiny in recent years.[71] However, COFI's proposal can be addressed, and to some extent discounted, on several fronts. First, although it would surely achieve clarity and certainty in respect of Crown and third party interests in land, the proposal does so by cutting historical aboriginal relationships with the earth. As Chief Edward John of the First Nations Summit of British Columbia noted:

> When government asks us to agree to surrender our title and agree to its extinguishment, they ask us to do away with our most basic sense of ourselves, and our relationship to the Creator, our territory and the other peoples of the worlds. We could no longer do that without agreeing that we no longer wish to exist as a distinct people. That is completely at odds with our intentions in negotiating treaties.[72]

In other words, COFI's proposal mirrors a certain tension between aboriginal understandings of aboriginal title and how it has been viewed traditionally by federal negotiators. On the one hand, aboriginal people see aboriginal title as referring to a set of inherent rights which define their basic sense of themselves and their relationship to the Creator, their territory, and the other peoples of the world. On the other hand, the COFI proposal sees aboriginal title as no more than a collection of quasi-property entitlements to use and enjoyment that can be traded once and for all to the Crown in return for treaty-based rights in respect of land governed by the treaty. Once the exchange occurs, aboriginal title can no longer exist in relation to land which has been surrendered, unless the treaty explicitly authorizes its continuation over certain geographic locations.

For aboriginal people, what treaties ought to do is not extinguish aboriginal title, but recognize it by agreement. On this basis, treaties should serve as solemn acts of mutual recognition of the ways that aboriginal people and Canadians structure their relationship to the land. Granted, it will not be possible in all cases for a treaty to reflect aboriginal understandings of aboriginal title. In Vancouver, for example, countervailing Crown and third party interests are probably far too entrenched. But in other areas, away from urban centres, the treaties should at least be able to set down certain aboriginal rights to land and governance that will be recognized by Canadian society and, in turn, to have certain Crown and third party rights to land recognized by the aboriginal community. In this manner, the treaty could provide the necessary bridge between aboriginal and

Canadian understandings of aboriginal title and thus serve as a vehicle of true co-existence.

Second, the COFI approach appears to run counter to the spirit and letter of the Royal Proclamation of 1763. Nothing in the text of the Proclamation points to outright surrenders of aboriginal title. Indeed, the overall thrust of the Proclamation is a Crown commitment to protect the ancestral lands of aboriginal peoples. As the text of the Proclamation makes clear: 'all Persons whatever who have either wilfully or inadvertently seated themselves upon any Lands ... which, not having been ceded or purchased by Us, as still reserved to the said Indians ... [are] strictly enjoin[ed] and require[d] ... to remove themselves.'[73] Thus, the Proclamation requires the Crown both to purchase aboriginal title and to protect lands subject to aboriginal title against encroachment.

Finally, not only does COFI's proposal appear to be based on an antiquated understanding of aboriginal rights as simple common law rights, it may even prevent treaties from evolving to meet new circumstances as the interests of the parties change over time. Most First Nations wish to negotiate treaties which include mechanisms for change. The Nuu'Chah'Nulth Tribal Council's negotiating position calls for the inclusion of such a mechanism in relation to certain treaty items. The Nisga'a AIP also contains a set of provisions outlining a rather elaborate dispute resolution process, which emphasizes consultation and cooperation between all parties to the agreement. Indeed, most contemporary arrangements between indigenous peoples and their former colonial states have incorporated into their treaties processes whereby change can occur.[74] The land claim agreement between the federal government and the Council of Yukon Indians, for example, contains provisions for ongoing negotiation and consultation among the parties.[75] COFI's proposal for the blanket extinguishment of aboriginal title, while plausible due to the certainty it creates in land interests, and indeed even justifiable on the basis of administrative expediency, precludes to a large extent a fluid relationship between First Nations and the Crown, yet flexibility has characterized treaty relationships between the Crown and aboriginal groups since the early period of colonization. To freeze the rights of aboriginal people for all time would also freeze the rights of successive provincial and federal governments. It would do everyone a disservice to foreclose the possibility for creative debate and solutions on future issues.

5
The Future of Treaty-Making

As various First Nations and both orders of government continue their negotiations into the latter half of the 1990s, a measure of uncertainty surrounds the future of treaty-making in British Columbia. The rise in the incidence of aboriginal blockades, heightened debate in Victoria due to public scrutiny of the Nisga'a AIP, and the concern about the pace of the negotiations have given birth to questions about the efficacy of the treaty process in addressing aboriginal grievances, and whether it should be changed to make it more inclusive of non-aboriginal interests. Have Native blockades put the treaty-making process in jeopardy? Do they point to a pervasive change in the manner in which Native groups express their grievances and in the way Native people perceive themselves within the dominant non-aboriginal society? What effect could such factors as political pressure and insufficient resources have on the treaty-making process and on the aboriginal groups participating in the negotiations?

A similar measure of uncertainty surrounds the consequences of the treaties themselves. While most of the negotiations are still at an early stage in the process, there has been little attention devoted to the question of who within aboriginal communities will benefit from the settlements. Will the advantages be shared by all? Or will they be confined largely to a select few who hold positions of authority within the new self-governing arrangements? Moreover, the way in which the treaties will be implemented has not been defined by either order of non-aboriginal government. Consequently, how do we determine whether the treaties will meet their desired objectives? Is there a role for the British Columbia Treaty Commission beyond its present treaty facilitating function in the post-ratification period of the treaties?

Aboriginal Protests
For the first two years of treaty talks, there were no incidents of Native

blockades in British Columbia. However, in the summer of 1995, the period of calm ended. In the interior of the province, a number of blockades involving the Okanagan and Shuswap First Nations were established. Unlike those of the late 1980s, which focused on more general grievances relating to unextinguished aboriginal rights, these blockades centred on the impact that commercial development was having on nearby reserve lands. The blockades were designed to impede non-aboriginal access to recreational areas and residential properties. The blockade at Douglas Lake was eventually dismantled, but only after the RCMP arranged to remove it and after the province's minister of aboriginal affairs agreed to set up negotiations with the Okanagan to deal with a series of their concerns.[1]

Later that summer, another blockade was erected at Gustafsen Lake, about 35 kilometres from 100 Mile House. It involved about thirty people who called themselves the 'Defenders of the Shuswap Nation.' The protesters received legal representation from Native rights lawyer Bruce Clark. While the area occupied was considered by the protesters to be sacred for the purpose of practising the sun dance, the legal argument underlying the occupation was presented by Clark in the opening pages of his book, *Native Liberty, Crown Sovereignty*:

> the imperial government of Great Britain in the eighteenth century recognized the liberty of the indigenous peoples not to be molested or disturbed on their unceded territories. This liberty received constitutional protection throughout British North America [by virtue of the Royal Proclamation of 1763]. The imperial government claimed overall sovereignty. Pursuant to that sovereignty it constituted the powers of the colonial governments. The powers delegated by the imperial government to these colonial governments were made to accommodate the previously recognized liberty of the natives. This constitutional pattern was never abrogated and thus, under the umbrella of crown sovereignty, it continues ... *The jurisdiction of federal and provincial governments to govern ceded territory is ... constitutionally counterbalanced – by the jurisdiction of the aboriginal peoples to govern themselves upon territory that they never voluntarily ceded.*[2] [emphasis added]

Accordingly, because much of British Columbia is not covered by treaties with the aboriginal people, Clark sought to bring the dispute to the attention of Queen Elizabeth, who could then approve an international court hearing in order to reaffirm aboriginal sovereignty in the area.

The position of those represented by Clark received little support from any circle. The provincial government chose to remain above the fray and to characterize the standoff as a criminal matter better left to the RCMP to resolve.[3] Many aboriginal groups distanced themselves from the position of the protesters, indicating that it ran counter to the peaceful traditions of the aboriginal people and that all disputes over land should be channelled through the current treaty negotiation process.[4] Moreover, from a legal perspective, one law professor suggested that the standoff was more of a political issue than one that could be resolved through litigation, since the courts had already ruled against the kind of argument put forward by Clark.[5] And others saw the legal basis for the protest as 'sheer lunacy,' which did little except 'add fuel to the fire' and was, for the most part, 'self-serving.'[6] Indeed, even the Supreme Court of Canada overruled Clark's legal argument. When Clark presented a motion to the Court asking the justices to decide whether the Court's jurisdiction over aboriginal people and their land was 'treasonable, fraudulent and genocidal,' the Court dismissed the motion and referred to Clark as a disgrace to the legal profession.

Such events would suggest the standoff at Gustafsen Lake had little direct effect on the legitimacy of the treaty-making process. None of the major players supported the goals of the protesters and, like the blockades erected in the interior of the province, the Gustafsen Lake blockade was seen generally as a peculiar expression of aboriginal discontent. However, Native blockades should not be dismissed out of hand; instead, they should draw our attention to some larger issues that could have serious implications for treaty-making. Regardless of whether they stem from unfulfilled promises of the federal government or from the alleged illegality of government action on unceded aboriginal land, blockades point to a sense of discontent amongst Native people over the manner in which Canadian governments have addressed aboriginal grievances. The history of aboriginal relations in British Columbia has shown that many coastal groups have pressed their claims for treaties and other items since the late 1880s with few tangible results. And as the Oka crisis of 1990 made clear to all, many Native people feel that Canadian governments only begin to take aboriginal grievances seriously when they are faced with blockades, violence, and other crisis situations. For many Native groups, following the more traditional avenues of litigation and negotiation is too time-consuming and creates little incentive for government to address Native issues in a timely fashion.

The blockades also reflect a more proactive approach by some aboriginal groups in dealing with government. Aboriginal people generally are no longer willing to accept the stereotype of Native people as victims of a world dominated by non-aboriginal interests. Yet they see their relatively small numbers and, for the most part, restricted access to the corridors of power as impediments to meaningful negotiations. Blockades and other forms of protest (e.g., rallies) are considered effective not only because they attract media attention, but also because they force government to act by presenting it with conflicting strategic options. If the government chooses to ignore a blockade, then the blockade is likely to continue and be used to restrict commercial development or the mobility of non-aboriginal people. Government inaction may also run the risk of producing an escalation in the conflict similar to the one at Oka. But by moving too quickly to address aboriginal demands, the government risks electoral condemnation and the potential of being perceived as weak and passively conceding to protesters, and thus inviting additional blockades. Thus, blockades and other acts of aboriginal protest present the government with the unenviable task of adopting a different political response to each specific situation.

Whether the ratification of treaties will put an end to the use of blockades is uncertain. But if treaties are concluded in an expeditious fashion, and if they are seen by aboriginal groups as fair and just, then there is at least the possibility that further blockades will be of limited value and viewed as illegitimate expressions of Native discontent. The treaties may demonstrate to Native groups not participating in treaty talks that progress can be made through negotiation as opposed to more conflictual avenues of expression. Indeed, neither Native nor non-Native people should be subject to an endless stream of Native protests. They polarize communities; they lead to intolerance among Natives and non-Natives alike; and they are not a productive use of human talent or of public and private funds.

Post-Election Environment:
Challenges Facing the NDP Government
At the time of this writing, an election had just been held in British Columbia. In the year leading up to the election, the NDP government adopted a hard-line approach to Native issues. Its declaration that only about 5 per cent of the province's land mass would be available as treaty settlement land and its decision to portray the Gustafsen Lake standoff as a criminal matter and not become significantly involved in the conflict is clear evidence of this approach. While the NDP was re-elected to another term of office by a small margin of legislative seats, the government will face a number of challenges in the years to come, as it attempts to negotiate treaties with aboriginal groups. Not only will the opposition parties in Victoria subject the Nisga'a AIP and any other agreements with First Nations to scrutiny, but there is the additional problem of providing adequate resources for the negotiations so that the treaties can be concluded in a reasonable period of time.

To consider the kind of scrutiny the treaties will face from the opposition parties, it may be useful to examine the positions taken by these parties prior to the election with regard to treaty negotiations. In June 1995 the leaders of the opposition parties were invited by various aboriginal groups on Vancouver Island to present their positions at a public meeting. Gordon Campbell (Liberal party leader) and Jack Weisgerber (Reform party leader) both indicated that the treaty-making process must continue in order to resolve the long-standing grievances of the province's aboriginal groups. But both leaders wished to see the process become more open, with greater public involvement in the talks and more public debate on the content of treaty settlements prior to their ratification by the government and the relevant First Nation.

The party leaders discussed the changes they would make to the treaty-making process if elected to office. While the Liberals would certainly continue to work toward the conclusion of treaties with First Nations, they would defend the interests of British Columbians 'more vigorously' than the NDP government. They would also ensure that laws would apply to aboriginal people and non-aboriginal people alike, though they failed to elaborate on this recommendation. Presumably it would entail forcing the federal government to modify or repeal some of the taxation provisions extended to aboriginal people, as evident in the Nisga'a AIP. The Liberals would discontinue the process of concluding all types of interim measures agreements with aboriginal groups, despite the implications such a move could have on the development of the region affected and the potential for further Native blockades. And they would allow local residents who may be affected by treaty settlements to join the negotiating teams, though it is not clear whether local residents would be allowed to offer submissions or simply be awarded observer status. Moreover, a Liberal government's negotiating position at the talks would be determined by the outcome of province-wide public hearings. Similar hearings would be held to debate the substance of treaty settlements prior to ratification by the parties involved.[7]

As might be expected, the Reform party proposed somewhat more extensive changes than those presented by the Liberal party. While supporting the alterations endorsed by the Liberals, the Reform party would subject all treaty settlements to a referendum in the particular region affected by the treaty. Under the current system, only aboriginal people vote directly on the contents of their treaty settlement. However, the Reform party would not ratify any agreement unless it met the approval of the local residents. For leader Jack Weisgerber, the reasoning behind the use of a popular vote was simple: 'If a proposed treaty is eminently fair and affordable, there should be no fear of putting it to a vote.'[8]

As attractive as Weisgerber's proposal might appear, it ignores the implications of using referenda to ratify treaty settlements. One the one hand, a referendum would likely stimulate public debate and involve more people in this stage of the negotiations. If binding, the outcome of the referendum would make the wishes of the majority of voters clear to both gov_rnments and the relevant First Nation. However, the thoughtful use of a referendum requires a well-informed voter who is able to make decisions on the basis of both the public good and self-interest. Treaty settlements involve issues which will have a direct impact on the welfare of many people. They also involve issues in which few individuals have a specialized or professional interest. In addition, our experiences with referenda in Canada and in Quebec suggest that the meaning and consequences of the question(s) put to the voter can be manipulated by politicians for political gain. And it is often the case that the information available to voters is shaped by powerful lobby groups, each with the promotion of their own interests in mind.[9] Moreover, Weisgerber's proposal for referenda does not include any indication of whether aboriginal people within a particular region would be allowed to vote. Nor does it address the question of whether a vote against a proposed treaty would end the negotiations once and for all, or whether the negotiations would recommence at a later date, with modifications to the provincial bargaining positions that would make the treaty settlement more palatable to those who initially rejected it.

Despite the kinds of changes to the process advocated by the opposition parties prior to the election, aboriginal treaties did not become an election issue. Only the Reform party attempted to introduce it into the campaign, suggesting once again that all such agreements with First Nations be put to a referendum in the region affected. This strategy was employed to gain voter support in the largely natural resource-based, small communities in the interior of the province, where opposition to treaties and support for the Reform party was relatively strong. Yet the Reform party's efforts went unchallenged: neither the Liberals nor the NDP wished to fight the election on the issue of aboriginal treaties. The Liberal party was already gathering some support in the interior region, so it would have been folly for them to campaign against treaties and risk losing their greater base of electoral support in the Vancouver area – an area where support for the treaty-making process was the strongest. The NDP simply had nothing to gain and everything to lose by raising the issue of treaties during the campaign. Indeed, the NDP did surprisingly well in areas where they were expected to do poorly, even winning the riding of Rupert – an area affected by the Nisga'a AIP – in large measure because they did not discuss aboriginal treaties during the campaign.

There is, however, an additional challenge facing the NDP government and, by extension, the treaty-making process: providing adequate revenue and personnel to conduct the negotiations in a timely fashion. Some negotiators of aboriginal groups involved in the process have argued that the provincial government is running the risk of scuttling the talks altogether by not contributing enough of these resources for the talks. Indeed, the main negotiators for the Lheit-Lit'en and Yekooche First Nations have recently made this claim and pointed out some potential consequences if the talks fail to make significant progress:

> they [the provincial government] are going to drive the process into the grave; they are not resourcing [the negotiations] adequately; the talks are bogging down, stalling. With 47 separate negotiations going on, our negotiations are lucky to get one day from the government each month. And it is not inconceivable that the benefits of the treaties will not be seen before the process begins to unravel. This will no doubt cause a great deal of dissension within native communities. Put this together with the recent failure of the NDP to protect many of the lands subject to claims from development through interim measure agreements, and you are going to see an explosion in Indian country. In fact, so much effort has gone into this process so far that if it fails what you will get is a backlash in native communities that will make the roadblocks of the 1980s look mild. [Standoffs such as] Oka will not be isolated incidents; they will be the norm.[10]

While defending treaties and conducting other negotiations expeditiously pose significant challenges to the NDP government, it is clear to all that the treaty-making process must continue. It would be disastrous for any incoming government to scuttle the talks or to introduce changes that would seriously impede the progress that has been made thus far. At the time of the election, some of the negotiations were close to or at the Agreement in Principle stage. This would stand as proof that the process begun in 1993 does indeed work. Any changes to the process that created a different playing field for those First Nations at a less advanced stage in their negotiations would be both unfair and possibly a source of political discontent. Instead of being seen as the precursor to the conclusion of solemn agreements between the Crown and aboriginal people, the negotiations would appear to First Nations as malleable and susceptible to the needs of political expediency. And in light of both the standoff at Gustafsen Lake and the attendant strong current of militancy which has coalesced among young aboriginal people around this event, it would be folly for any new provincial government to ignore the impact that altering the process may have on Native people.

At the same time, third party interests and the general public will probably not tolerate the continuation of negotiations which consign them to a role of observing negotiations and providing input which, by some accounts, has fallen on deaf ears. The non-aboriginal population will also become less tolerant of Native blockades, which may gain momentum with increased publicity, and this lack of public tolerance will not be conducive to resolution through negotiation. In short, the newly re-elected NDP government will face a difficult task as the 1990s wear on: it will have to balance the interests of all sides, all the while attempting to make the process less expensive, more efficient, and more accountable to non-aboriginal people and third party interests.

The Outcome of Modern Treaties
Much of the dialogue on the forthcoming treaties in the province has focused on the negotiating process, with little discussion of the outcome of the treaties themselves. To a large extent the absence of debate on this aspect of the treaties is not surprising, since many of the negotiations are still at an early stage. Nevertheless, it might be instructive to offer some thoughts on issues that are likely to arise once the settlements have been ratified.

Who Will Benefit from Treaty Settlements?
Traditional aboriginal leaders were the servants of their people. The values of reciprocity, redistribution, and consensus-building were held to be paramount. However, with the imposition of the band council system as it is set out in the Indian Act, hierarchical authority was delegated to aboriginal leaders from the Department of Indian Affairs, placing leaders in the position of acting as managers of their people. In many cases, traditional systems of aboriginal leadership were transformed into a ruling-class system. And government officials exploited the absence of Western-style forms of political organization in aboriginal communities through a practice of political and economic favouritism toward certain families who were willing to ally themselves with the Canadian government. Goods and services to bands were funnelled through these families, who in turn gave themselves and their followers a disproportionate amount of benefits.[11]

At first most aboriginal groups resisted or were at least apathetic to the provisions in the Indian Act regarding elected band councils. Despite this, factional disputes within aboriginal communities did occur between traditionalists and those who favoured the band council system, which proved bothersome to the Department of Indian Affairs. In response, the department decided to allow certain bands to select leaders in the traditional manner, as long as the chief complied with the authority of the department. However, if a particular band showed signs of resistance, the department's Indian agent on the reserve would select and appoint the chief and councillors, and then channel the department's benefits and authority through these appointees. Indeed, when Parliament amended the Indian Act in the 1880s to provide for the election of a chief and council, it was probably motivated to a large extent by the desire to gain more control over aboriginal people by removing all remnants of their traditional systems of government. To be sure, the Act's amendment still gave bands a choice in their form of governance, but for all intents and purposes, the option of adopting a so-called 'customary' approach to government was only a variation of the band council system. The band council system also conformed to the standard electoral system in Canada in many respects. The candidate with a simple plurality of votes gains the position of leader. Thus, the process favoured candidates from the largest kin groups; smaller kin groups were alienated, leading often to divisions within the aboriginal community between the those who ruled and those who did not.[12]

These kinds of changes to the governance of aboriginal communities gave rise not only to an aboriginal ruling class, but also to an elite aboriginal socio-economic class. Thus, on most reserves there continue to be two socio-economic classes: a small, virtually closed, elite group, which includes influential landowners, politicians, bureaucrats, and a few entrepreneurs; and a large lower class, comprised of destitute and powerless people. Because unemployment hovers around 60 to 90 per cent on most reserves, and it is employment that generally gives rise to a transitional or middle class, there is no intermediate socio-economic stratum on most reserves. One of the consequences of this social division is a corresponding division of political and economic interests, with the elite class controlling the political agenda to the detriment of the lower class. And this dichotomy manifests itself in the interests pursued by the aboriginal leadership: expansions of jurisdiction and control over band political and administrative structures are pursued, while little attention is given to the problems affecting the lower class, such as unemployment, alcohol abuse, and high rates of suicide and incarceration. This is not to suggest that these problems do not receive any attention from aboriginal leaders, but rather that they may not receive the attention and collective action necessary to solve them.[13] Indeed, most aboriginal people are aware of these divisions within reserve-based communities. And, as aboriginal people articulated in response to the involvement of Ovide Mercredi in the 1995 standoffs in British Columbia and in Ontario, those aboriginal people outside the power elite may not wish to tolerate this situation much longer:

> To the ordinary First Nations person, the elected First Nations leadership has evolved into a complacent entity totally dependent on the government teat. What is being said is that the endless negotiations occupying the political agenda are benefiting the wrong people. It is now time for Mr. Mercredi and the other mainstream leaders to step aside and make room for more determined resistance to violation of our rights.[14]

On this basis, the kinds of self-governing arrangements that are included in treaty settlements should move away from the authority structures of the band council system. Elements of the more traditional systems of governance, and the values they sought to protect, should be allowed to blossom, as they are in the self-government provisions of the Nisga'a AIP. Those aboriginal people at the lower end of the socio-economic scale deserve more than what has been given to them in the past. Like Canadians generally, aboriginal people are becoming less deferential to authority and less willing to have an elite cadre of individuals control their lives. They are also less willing to see those holding positions of authority – often acquired through less than fair means – reap benefits from those positions at the expense of others.

The federal proposals on self-government may be too restrictive to allow this kind of re-evolution in traditional forms of aboriginal government to occur. But at the very least the band council provisions of the Indian Act should be repealed. Perhaps even the eventual dismantling of both the Department of Indian Affairs, and of provincial departments charged with the regulation and administration of all but the most essential services to aboriginal communities, must also be considered seriously if the various forms of aboriginal self-government are to be responsive to the citizens they govern. Indeed, in a recent study at the Kennedy School of Government at Harvard University, Joseph Kalt found that as the regulatory and administrative ties between the federal government and various Indian Nations in the United States were dismantled, the overall living standard of Native people tended to rise. When Indian Nations became less reliant on the federal government, the 'demoralizing spiral of co-dependency' also began to erode.[15] As Kalt notes: 'The fate of the BIA [Bureau of Indian Affairs] rises and falls with the fate of Indian country . . . The higher the unemployment rate, the worse the poverty, the better off the BIA; its budget rises, its staff rises, its power rises.'[16] Thus, tribes who are more responsible for their own affairs will tend to be more economically prosperous. Those tribes who do not follow this approach and rather 'pin their hopes on more federal dollars and lawsuits over lost land will still be poor after the money and title arrive.'[17] The key is therefore less interference from the federal government and more effective self-government.

Determining Whether Treaties Have Met Their Goals

Discussions about treaty outcomes in terms of what they ought to accomplish are difficult to avoid because neither order of non-aboriginal government has indicated how they expect the treaties to fulfil their desired goals. For example, COFI noted recently that the provincial government's goal of concluding treaties which are 'affordable' and 'fair' 'gives the impression [that the government's position] is more of a wish list of what government might *like* treaties to do than a realistic strategy of *how* they will accomplish it.'[18] As one former high-ranking federal official noted, the provincial government's inability to indicate how it will achieve the objectives of the treaties can be attributed to a reluctance by governments generally to have their policies scrutinized prior to implementation, or evaluated later on the basis of success or failure.[19] Victoria's paramount concern at this point in the treaty talks is less than thorough or scientific: rather than indicating the general goals of the treaties and then moving to a more specific set of standards by which these general goals can be met, the provincial government's objective is simply to reach an agreement with an aboriginal group, or be seen as making some progress in the talks.[20] If this view is accurate, then it would follow that little credence has been given to such activities as assessing the viability of aboriginal economic development initiatives included in the treaties. In short, 'the process has become politicized, with very little concern given to rigorous forms of analysis.'[21]

This weakness in the government's approach to the negotiations is unfortunate, because it asks those not involved in treaty talks directly to place a great deal of faith in the decisions of the negotiators. Yet formal analyses can be used once treaties have been concluded. This could allow both orders of non-aboriginal government, non-aboriginal people, and aboriginal groups to see for themselves the outcome of the treaties in terms of their benefits and costs. Such analyses should be considered a natural part of the treaty-making process. Indeed, other jurisdictions involved in Native land claims have used such techniques. In the United States, for example, a treaty impact analysis was performed in relation to Native timber harvested in the Tongass National Forest as a consequence of the Alaska Native Claims Settlement Act of 1971. The Act established thirteen Native corporations in southeast Alaska, which were allowed to select approximately 540,000 acres (218,530 hectares) of timber out of the land conveyed by the Act. The study found that Native timber harvests, which began in the late 1970s, grew rapidly during the late 1980s. But by 1991 most of the Native corporations had harvested all of their merchantantable timber. The study concluded that, if market conditions continued unchanged, Native harvests would decline continuously for the next ten to fifteen years.[22]

A failure to use a similar kind of analysis in relation to some of the economic development goals of the treaties in British Columbia would be unfortunate. It would be disappointing to all concerned if the treaties failed to offer Native groups the chance to become economically self-sufficient or to encourage aboriginal groups to diversify their holdings by pursuing other ventures. Moreover, treaty impact analyses may even allow the terms of treaties to be altered to meet some future needs of the parties, and thus enable the settlements to become 'living documents.'

Addressing Treaty-Related Grievances in British Columbia
The use of treaty impact analyses is one way of ensuring the treaties can meet their goals. Also important to their implementation is the vehicle by which treaty-related grievances can be channelled and addressed. The six stage process of concluding a treaty does not indicate a role for the British Columbia Treaty Commission past the treaty ratification stage. Its mandate is only to facilitate the negotiation and conclusion of the treaties. Once all of the treaties have been concluded in the province, the commission will presumably cease to exist. It will fall to the federal Indian Claims Commission to address the treaty-related grievances of British Columbia's aboriginal groups.

Created in 1991, the Indian Claims Commission acts as an independent and impartial body, charged with the authority to address disputes arising out of the 'specific claims' process.[23] Comprised of aboriginal and non-aboriginal commissioners, the commission undertakes inquiries and offers mediation to the parties involved in a specific claim. Inquiries occur either when the claim of an aboriginal group is rejected by the federal government, or when it has been accepted, but there is disagreement over the compensation criteria applied to resolve the claim. The inquiries contain a series of stages that result in a formal report of the commission's recommendations, based on the findings made during the inquiry. The recommendations of the commission are not binding on either the aboriginal group or the federal government. With the consent of the relevant aboriginal group, inquiries are held in the aboriginal community, and allow evidence to be submitted by elders and community members. Mediation can occur at any point during the specific claim process in order to ensure the continuation of the negotiations. With the assistance of the commission, it is the responsibility of the parties to work out the form of mediation that best meets the needs of their particular dispute.[24]

Submitting a claim to the commission does not preclude an aboriginal group from opening or continuing negotiations with the federal government or with other organizations over any issue relating to the claim. Sometimes, however, the federal government will unilaterally suspend negotiations following a request by an aboriginal group for an inquiry. Moreover, the submission of a claim does not prevent an aboriginal group from taking their claim to court. Indeed, even if litigation has been commenced, a claim can be sent to the commission. Yet the legal action will be considered by the commission when it determines the most appropriate action to take to resolve a dispute. For example, the commission may not schedule a community inquiry at the same time a trial is in progress or release a report while a court decision is pending on the same issue.[25]

Other jurisdictions have in place similar bodies to address treaty-related grievances by aboriginal groups. For example, in New Zealand, the Waitangi Tribunal performs a similar role of addressing alleged treaty violations of the Treaty of Waitangi of 1840. Created by legislation in 1975, the tribunal is directed to hear any claim by any Maori individual or group that some action of the Crown has been prejudicial to them and has been in conflict with the principles of the Treaty of Waitangi of 1840. The tribunal is responsible for making recommendations to the government on such claims and is given the exclusive right to interpret the treaty, taking into account both its English and Maori versions.[26]

The tribunal is staffed by seven members. Four members must be of Maori descent. Two must be non-Maori, and not necessarily lawyers. The final member of the tribunal is the chief judge of the Maori Land Court. The tribunal holds its hearings at a *marae* (i.e., a meeting place with spiritual significance for the Maori person or tribe making the claim), and it tries to incorporate into its deliberations *kawa* (i.e., Maori customs and methods of discussion), thus allowing the tribunal to conduct its proceedings in a manner which is familiar to its clients.[27]

Because its recommendations are not legally binding on the government, the tribunal's efficacy in resolving treaty-related claims is wholly dependent upon the government's compliance. In most cases, the government has adhered to the recommendations of the tribunal. When there has been some initial reluctance to do so, the government has altered its decision in the face of public pressure.[28] The tribunal is seen as legitimate in the eyes of the Maori, and increasingly so in those of the Pakeha, or non-Maori. Opposition to Maori claims from Pakeha circles centres more on the contemporary application of the Treaty of Waitangi of 1840 rather than on the work of the tribunal itself.[29]

Institutions such as the Indian Claims Commission and the Waitangi Tribunal are important to the resolution of aboriginal claims. Their ability to offer mediation and to conduct investigations into alleged treaty or statutory violations by the Crown affords a measure of informality, cultural sensitivity, and flexibility into the resolution of disputes – characteristics not often found in the judicial forum. Litigation is adversarial by its very nature and largely controlled by the parties.[30] It also imposes significant empirical demands on courts, particularly in terms of data gathering, which courts are not well equipped to undertake. Judicial decisions are too principle prone and too principle bound, and deal case by case with too narrow a slice of reality.[31] In contrast, the recommendations of institutions such as commissions and tribunals are not binding on the parties, which allows the parties to fashion mutually acceptable outcomes and to arrive at decisions which make them accountable to their respective constituencies. By conducting their proceedings in the aboriginal community affected by the dispute and by allowing the participation of elders and community members, the work of these institutions should be seen as legitimate in the eyes of aboriginal people. In short, they are bodies which take account of the complex nature of aboriginal grievances and provide ways to resolve these disputes with which both parties can live. They should be seen as a vital part of the implementation of aboriginal treaties.

Conclusion

A number of general questions were posed at the outset of this book concerning both the process of treaty-making and the final treaty settlements themselves. Because many pages have passed, and a range of rejoinders offered, it is necessary to summarize. This will allow the book to conclude in a coherent fashion and will offer to the reader a clear understanding of the treaty aspect of the Indian land question in British Columbia.

The reasons for negotiating treaties with aboriginal groups are grounded in a combination of legal requirements, political imperatives, and historical precedents. When the explorers and settlers from the various European Nations arrived on the shores of the Pacific coast they came upon culturally diverse and politically sophisticated groups of aboriginal people. Like Europeans, the indigenous peoples had formal structures of government, complex languages, ways of classifying themselves, and well-defined territories. Doubtless there were also differences from Europeans in the forms of sociopolitical organization maintained by coastal and interior peoples, but aboriginal laws, institutions of government, and hunting and fishing practices have been recognized, by the common law doctrine of aboriginal rights, as pre-existing rights that have survived assertions of sovereignty by the British Crown. Significantly, this common law method of maintaining corresponding laws and institutions was based on a desire by the British to allow for the peaceful co-existence of several nations over the same land.

This spirit of peaceful co-existence also coloured one means by which both international law and British policy mandated territorial acquisition and the assertion of British sovereignty during the 1800s. In cases where there were pre-existing societies of indigenous peoples holding specific territories, the method to be used was cession. This would require the consent of the aboriginal people to the transfer of some or all of their lands to the British Crown. The new relationship would be codified in the form of a treaty. The British Crown was then required to pay some form of compensation to the Native people in exchange for what they had ceded. This approach was followed by the British in other colonies; it was the method advocated by the Hudson's Bay Company in relation to the settlement of parts of Vancouver Island; and it was the method followed by Governor Douglas when he arranged fourteen purchase treaties with aboriginal groups on Vancouver Island.

However, although the federal government continued to conclude treaties with aboriginal groups in other parts of Canada, the practice was discontinued in Vancouver Island, with no treaties arranged after 1854. The reasons for this are varied. On the one hand, all three levels of governmental authority in the colony of Vancouver Island (the Colonial Office, the governor of the colony, the legislative assembly in Victoria) placed the onus on the other to arrange treaties. Yet nothing was done. On the other hand, there was also a change in the colony's policy respecting aboriginal people. Unlike earlier times, colonial policy now had a clearly assimilationist thrust, designed to integrate Native people into the mainstream of the emerging white society. Aboriginal title was denied, so there was no need for treaties. The treaties arranged by Douglas on Vancouver Island were characterized as simple friendship agreements, perhaps even commendable devices for placating the Native people. And the reserves set aside for aboriginal groups were seen by colonial officials as mere gifts, not as a recognition of the pre-existence of aboriginal land rights, or as the result of a surrender by Natives of the land adjacent to their reserves.

These views remained relatively constant throughout the 1900s, as both Victoria and Ottawa did little to assist the Native people in their plight. In fact, it is more accurate to suggest that both governments did what they could to subjugate the Native population. The demands by coastal chiefs and others for treaties, larger reserve lands, and self-government were cast aside by provincial officials, who regarded them as a disguised ploy for more land. The federal government for its part prohibited the potlatch and any other aboriginal ceremony that involved the exchange of goods, material, or money. And many activities relating to claims activity by Native people were also disallowed. Aboriginal people and their demands were seen as problems, better left ignored or discredited. And they were certainly not a constituency that could command the attention of either order of government.

However, during the late 1960s and into the 1970s, the tide began to turn. The political organizations that aboriginal people had formed to assert their claims had gained strength, and many began to use litigation to force the provincial and federal legislators to adopt a more enlightened aboriginal policy. Indeed, if there was one motivating force behind the initiation of the current treaty-making process in the province, it was the cumulative effect of court rulings on the aboriginal policies of Victoria and Ottawa. Beginning with the *Calder* decision in 1973 and culminating in the *Delgamuukw* decision in 1993, aboriginal people would be awarded legal victories which gave them a strong foundation on which their subsequent dealings with both orders of government could operate. In *Calder*, the Supreme Court of Canada held that aboriginal title pre-existed the assertion of British sovereignty in British Columbia. The same Court in *Guerin* held not only that aboriginal title was a pre-existing right based on Native peoples' historic occupation and possession of their tribal lands, but that it had force both on reserve land and on traditional tribal lands not subject to treaties. And in *Delgamuukw* the British Columbia Court of Appeal ruled that aboriginal people had unextinguished, non-exclusive aboriginal rights over their traditional tribal territories. These rights were protected both by the common law and by the Constitution Act of 1982. More importantly, the Court in *Delgamuukw* stated that it was incumbent upon governments to negotiate the precise location, scope, and content of these aboriginal rights; the judicial forum was not the proper venue for the determination of such questions.

The rulings of the courts, along with popular opinion and the views of major natural resource development companies, were sufficient to alter the traditional policy position of the British Columbia government regarding treaties and their negotiation. Aboriginal people had pre-existing rights in certain sections of the province, which had not been dealt with adequately by government. The stage was thus set to begin a process of treaty negotiations never attempted before in any province on such a large scale.

The process for negotiating the treaties is noteworthy because it has been designed as a logical means for the public and other interested parties, as well as the actual parties to the negotiations, to measure the progress of the talks. The six-stage process is intended to prevent the occurrence of negotiations on an ad hoc basis, and it enables each aboriginal group to negotiate a treaty on the basis of established rules and criteria.

Judging from the number of aboriginal groups participating in the negotiations, it seems that most look upon the process favourably. However, some First Nations, particularly those belonging to the Union of British Columbia Indian Chiefs, have refused to participate. They view the treaty process as illegitimate, since it involves negotiations over rights to land and resources that have never been formally ceded by aboriginal groups to any order of Canadian government. Among non-aboriginal people, criticism of the negotiations centres on the quality of third party and public involvement in the talks. For example, participants in TNAC regard their role in the negotiations as peripheral and view the committee as a means devised by government of reassuring the public that the negotiations are not being conducted in secrecy and at the expense of non-aboriginal interests. While more of TNAC's specific criticism will be discussed below, it is important to emphasize that the public and third party interests will be offered a greater opportunity to witness, and to some extent participate in, the formation of treaties during the latter stages of the treaty-making process, as the issues subject to negotiation become more tangible.

There are some interesting implications associated with the cost-sharing agreement between Ottawa and Victoria as set out in the MOU. First, off-loading between the two orders of government is proscribed. Unless agreed to previously by Ottawa and Victoria, any treaty provision which results in the transfer of additional costs to another government is prohibited. This provision in the MOU should prevent much of the off-loading the federal government has undertaken in recent years in policy areas that are subject to shared jurisdiction with the provinces. It should also serve as a check against the provincial government assuming a preponderance of the policy responsibilities over aboriginal affairs once the treaties have been ratified. Apart from where there is a devolution of power to First Nations as a result of the treaties, the policy authority will be shared by the federal and British Columbia governments.

The federal government appears to bear much of the cost of concluding treaties, although there may be some significant costs for the province, particularly through lost revenues as a consequence of the transfer of Crown lands to First Nations. However, it should be remembered that many aboriginal groups have expressed their displeasure over the land selection model used in the negotiations, since some of this land appears to be of little commercial value. If the provincial Crown lands involved in negotiations are less valuable than other Crown lands, then the loss in potential revenue might be less than it would be if more valuable lands were transferred. It is not clear whether the land selection model is a deliberate strategy on the part of the provincial government to reduce overall losses in revenues. In addition, while Ottawa will absorb the total costs of providing loans to First Nations for their negotiations, if a First Nation defaults on a loan, the provincial government is responsible for a sizable portion of the loan in default.

While many of the negotiations have yet to tackle the operational requirements of the issues involved in the treaty talks, some tentative observations can be made. Awarding treaty settlement land (i.e., land beyond that which is currently held as reserve land) to urban-based First Nations will be difficult, due to its high market value and its relative scarcity in areas such as Vancouver. Consequently, the cash component of their settlement packages will probably be greater than that offered to First Nations in rural areas or in areas where third party interests are less prevalent. This suggests that if urban-based First Nations, such as the Squamish, wish to expand their current reserve lands, they will have to use the cash component of their settlement to purchase land near their reserves, just as a private land developer. Consequently, treaty settlements offered to First Nations will pose little, if any, threat to fee simple title holders in the province. Only if fee simple title holders wish to sell their interest will this form of private property be part of treaty settlements.

There is an express desire by government negotiators to design treaty settlements that accommodate the needs and concerns of specific First Nations. But there may be some difficulty associated with maintaining this diversity. Like the Sechelt, many First Nations have indicated they will not accept treaty settlements that give another First Nation a higher per capita settlement. Such statements may simply be the sort of rhetoric found in most negotiations. But if they represent a non-negotiable position, this could present difficulties for government negotiators as talks proceed to the Agreement in Principle stage. If each First Nation accepts no less than that what is offered to another First Nation, both orders of government will face the problem of rising expectations, which could pose a threat to the expeditious conclusion of treaties.

While it is relatively safe to assume that title held in fee simple will not be a direct part of the treaty negotiations, other forms of private property, such as timber and agricultural leases on Crown land, could be. The treaty-making goals of increasing aboriginal management authority in the natural resource sector and developing aboriginal economic initiatives do contemplate some degree of interference with these types of land holdings. Indeed, if the Nisga'a AIP and New Zealand's land claim negotiations with various Maori tribes are any indications, Crown land leases held by private resource development corporations could be purchased by government to conclude a treaty.

The jurisdictional reach of aboriginal self-government and the manner in which it will exist alongside the legislative powers of Canadian governments appears quite limited. As a result, the federal government's proposal on aboriginal self-government has not been welcomed by many First Nations, if any. It is rather less than the position Ottawa initially set forth in the talks, and indeed is considerably less than the federal and other provincial governments were willing to accept as part of the constitutional amendments contained in the Charlottetown Accord of 1992. Consequently, the ultimate nature and scope of aboriginal self-government will doubtless be subject to heated debate as the treaty negotiations proceed.

As regards the major non-aboriginal sources of opposition to treaty-making during the first two years of the negotiations, concerns about secrecy have been addressed by both levels of government and by some First

Nations, although not entirely to the satisfaction of members of TNAC. Specifically, TNAC has argued that:

- The provincial government continues to conclude interim measures agreements with First Nations on an ad hoc basis without meaningful input from third party interests.
- Government negotiators have not offered TNAC any satisfying explanation of aboriginal rights or the inherent right of self-government.
- Government negotiators have not always received a clear mandate to negotiate certain items.
- Government and First Nation negotiators have forged agreement on certain matters before any third party consultation occurs.
- When the views of TNAC are solicited, TNAC is given little time to respond.

Clearly, third party interests and the concerns of the public should have a more substantive impact on the final treaty settlements during the Framework Agreement and Agreement in Principle stages. This is not to suggest that the process for outside consultation prior to and during these stages is by any means perfect; indeed, many feel that the process should be altered in some way so as to allow those outside government and aboriginal communities a greater say in the negotiation of the treaties. But if such a change to the process does occur, it must be carried out with a great deal of care and must incorporate the views of First Nations. It would be unfortunate, and ultimately serve no purpose, to amend the process in a manner that allowed the negotiations to be undermined for reasons based on prejudice and bias alone.

The cost of settling treaties will be sizable. Presently over $30 million has been spent on the negotiations, which includes the costs of developing policy positions and relocating government officials. Not included in this figure is the $15 million provided to First Nations for their participation in the negotiations. However, in terms of the monetary value of individual treaty settlement packages, most eyes will continue to be fixed on the Nisga'a AIP. Once the AIP is implemented, both orders of government envision the cost of the Nisga'a treaty to be approximately $357 million, comprising land, cash, and cash equivalents. But these costs must be placed in a particular context. Primarily, they are the costs of living up to our legal obligations to aboriginal groups as a result of discontinuing the practice of concluding treaties in the 1850s. They are also the costs required to end aboriginal people's long-standing dependency on government and give them the means to participate in the economy of the province as semi-independent entities. Moreover, the costs of treaty settlements will be dispersed over a period of approximately twenty years and be absorbed as part of government's overall expenditures. In short, the costs of concluding treaties should be seen not only as a legal and moral imperative, but also as a more effective way of allocating funds to aboriginal groups than has been employed over the past century.

The federal and provincial governments are not negotiating treaty settlements which contravene the British Columbia Court of Appeal's 1993 decision in *Delgamuukw*. Indeed, the governments' respective negotiating positions are consistent with the Court's directive to determine the extent to which unextinguished aboriginal rights and those of third parties can co-exist on Crown land. Moreover, it should be emphasized that governments often legislate in policy fields in ways that go beyond the strict requirements of the law. This is simply what governance requires. There is no abrogation of the rule of law as long as what government does is not illegal. If a segment of the population objects to certain governmental acts or practices, then it is entitled to voice these concerns and attempt to change government policy through a variety of democratic channels.

The recent Native blockades, the political opposition to aboriginal treaties, and the matter of providing sufficient resources for the negotiations were all considered in relation to their effect on the treaty-making process. All of the blockades were resolved without fatalities. Yet the standoff at Gustafsen Lake particularly underscored the desire of both the provincial government and the major First Nations in the blockade area to do nothing that would undermine the efficacy of the treaty-making process in resolving Native claims. The provincial government characterized the standoff as a criminal matter, best left to the RCMP for resolution. And the First Nations suggested that all grievances be channelled through the treaty-making process. Only a handful of Native supporters applauded the actions of the protesters. In short, all the major players were onside, and the overall legitimacy of the treaty-making process emerged untouched. Perhaps a violent end to the standoff would have been welcomed by some non-Natives, since it would have illustrated their belief that treaty negotiations are fruitless. But a violent end could have spawned a whole host of other protests, either similar to the one at Gustafsen Lake or opposing the use of violence by the RCMP. Thus, the provincial government could not have pursued or encouraged any other means of resolution. And despite the media's efforts to downplay the significance of a nonviolent conclusion to the standoff (instead they emphasized its overall cost to taxpayers), all involved should be commended for their restraint. A violent end to the dispute would have done nothing except inflame the passions of Native and non-Native people alike, and would have done much to discredit the treaty negotiations.

Yet Native blockades also point to a general feeling of discontent by aboriginal people over the manner in which Canadian governments have traditionally addressed Native grievances. The history of Native relations in British Columbia has shown that many aboriginal groups have petitioned the provincial government to negotiate treaties since the 1880s, with few substantive results. And while litigation has been an effective means of achieving recognition of legal rights for aboriginal groups, judicial decisions themselves have not always induced governments to act. Consequently, blockades and other crisis situations seem to be a most effective means of forcing governments to take Native claims seriously, and they suggest, by extension, that aboriginal people are no longer willing to accept the stereotype of themselves as victims in a society dominated largely by non-aboriginal interests. Also, a blockade is an effective tool to induce government to act. Not only does it attract a healthy measure of media attention, but it can also place government in an embarrassing and sensitive position strategically, requiring a delicate balancing of aboriginal and non-aboriginal interests. To what extent these acts of civil disobedience will continue in the future, perhaps even after the treaties are concluded, is uncertain. But if blockades are to be used less often by aboriginal groups, and if they are to be seen as illegitimate expressions of aboriginal discontent, then the treaties must be concluded expeditiously and be seen as fair and just, especially by Native groups.

Even though the NDP emerged victorious in the 1996 provincial election, some procedural changes to the process of treaty-making will occur. These will involve making the negotiations less costly, more inclusive of non-aboriginal and third party interests, and more efficient. Indeed, expediting the negotiations is important, particularly for aboriginal groups, since some have expressed discontent over the rate at which the talks have proceeded recently. Other, more substantive alterations would create a sense of inconsistency in the negotiations and could serve to stall the talks even more. In other words, it will be important to ensure that any reconstruction of the process does not create a different set of rules for those First Nations at a less advanced stage. This would be unfair; it would also send a clear message to the First Nations that the process is so adaptable that it can be altered on the basis of political expediency.

The outcome of the treaties has been considered in the light of three questions: Who within the aboriginal community will benefit from the treaty settlements? How do we determine whether the treaties have met their goals? And what could be the future role of the British Columbia Treaty Commission once the treaties have been concluded? The benefits of treaty settlements should be dispersed throughout the aboriginal communities to which they apply. It would be unfortunate if the settlements created a replication of the socio-economic class stratification that occurred within many Native communities as a result of the band council provisions of the Indian Act. Indeed, there are signs that the legitimacy of some elected aboriginal leaders is in serious doubt. However, whether a return to more traditional systems of aboriginal government can correct these problems quickly is debatable. Many years have passed since traditional forms of government were in operation. Aboriginal communities have changed both socially and politically. The imprint of the band council system of government may be too deep to allow an unfettered blossoming of traditional forms of government. Nevertheless, despite the federal government's proposal regarding the nature and scope of self-government (a proposal which may be too restrictive to allow anything but quasi-municipal forms of government to emerge within Native communities), it might be prudent for treaty negotiators to attempt to revive at least some elements of the traditional forms of Native rule.

These assertions about what the treaties ought to do once they have been concluded suggests the provincial government has done little to provide the public with precise indications of how the treaties will accomplish their goals. Both the experiences of other jurisdictions involved in land claims and formal methods of analysis may be useful in adding a measure of certainty to the process. The lack of clarity by the provincial government in setting forth the operational requirements of treaty objectives has forced those outside the negotiations to place their faith in the hands of the negotiators, for a positive outcome in the treaties.

Once all of the treaties have been concluded in the province, the British Columbia Treaty Commission should cease to exist. The objective of the commission was to facilitate treaty negotiations. There is no role for it during the implementation phase of the treaties. Consequently, the Indian Claims Commission will serve as the vehicle by which alleged violations of treaties by the Crown can be resolved. Its ability to offer mediation and to conduct investigations into aboriginal grievances allows a healthy measure of flexibility and cultural sensitivity to be incorporated into the resolution of these disputes. And since its recommendations are not binding on the parties, both sides can arrive at mutually acceptable outcomes. Although one hopes that the Indian Claims Commission will not be called upon too often after treaties in British Columbia are concluded, its role will be a vital and legitimate component of treaty implementation.

The overall impact of the treaties will not be known for some time. Despite some of the problems associated with the process of treaty-making, it appears to be a worthwhile endeavour. Ultimately, its aim is to work out mutually acceptable and beneficial relationships between aboriginal and non-aboriginal people and their governments, and to allow aboriginal communities to acquire a degree of political autonomy so they can partic-ipate to a greater extent in the economy of British Columbia. Only when aboriginal groups become more self-sufficient can the ties that bind them to government be cut. However, it must be emphasized that non-aborigi-nal people do not have to accept as positive every aspect of the treaty-mak-ing process. Some of it deserves to be questioned and to be reformed. Hopefully, this book will help to facilitate some debate about the merits and pitfalls of negotiating treaties. It should also be emphasized that choosing not to conclude treaties will do little to eradicate the factors which gave rise to the treaty-making process in the first place. Unextin-guished aboriginal rights will remain; injunctions by the courts could con-tinue to be issued, thus impeding natural resource development; Native blockades may be erected as expressions of Native discontent; and a mea-sure of economic instability in the province will continue. In the end, one hopes that treaties will give rise to aboriginal communities that, while more independent, interact meaningfully with the non-aboriginal popula-tion of British Columbia.

Appendixes

Appendix A: Recommendations of the British Columbia Claims Task Force, 1991

The British Columbia Claims Task Force recommended that:

1 The First Nations, Canada, and British Columbia establish a new relationship based on mutual trust, respect, and understanding – through political negotiations.
2 Each of the parties be at liberty to introduce any issue at the negotiation table which it views as significant to the new relationship.
3 A British Columbia Treaty Commission be established by agreement among the First Nations, Canada, and British Columbia to facilitate the process of negotiations.
4 The commission consist of a full-time chairperson and four commissioners – of whom two are appointed by the First Nations, and one each by the federal and provincial governments.
5 A six-stage process be followed in negotiating treaties.
6 The treaty negotiation process be open to all First Nations in British Columbia.
7 The organization of First Nations for the negotiations is a decision to be made by each First Nation.
8 First Nations resolve issues related to overlapping traditional territories among themselves.
9 Federal and provincial governments start negotiations as soon as First Nations are ready.
10 Non-aboriginal interests be represented at the negotiating table by the federal and provincial governments.
11 The First Nation, Canadian, and British Columbian negotiating teams be sufficiently funded to meet the requirements of the negotiations.
12 The commission be responsible for allocating funds to the First Nations.
13 The parties develop ratification procedures which are confirmed in the Framework Agreement and in the Agreement in Principle.
14 The commission provide advice and assistance in dispute resolution as agreed by the parties.
15 The parties select skilled negotiators and provide them with a clear mandate, and training as required.
16 The parties negotiate interim measures agreements before or during the treaty negotiations when an interest is being affected which could undermine the process.
17 Canada, British Columbia, and the First Nations jointly undertake public education and information programs.
18 The parties in each negotiation jointly undertake a public information program.
19 British Columbia, Canada, and the First Nations request the First Nations Education Secretariat, and various educational organizations in British Columbia, to prepare resource materials for use in the schools and by the public.

Appendix B: Aboriginal Groups Participating in Treaty Negotiations in British Columbia (as of April 1996)

Cariboo Tribal Council
Carrier-Sekani Tribal Council and Cheslatta Carrier Nation
Champagne & Aishihik First Nations
Ditidaht First Nation
Esketemic Nation (Alkali Lake)
Gitanyow Hereditary Chiefs
Gitxsan
Haida Nation
Haisla Nation (Kitamaat)
Heiltsuk Nation
Homalco Band
Hul'qumi'num Speaking Peoples
In-Shuck-Ch
Kaska Dene Council
Katzie Indian Band
Klahoose Nation
Ktunaxa Nation
Kwakiutl First Nations
Lheit-Lit'en Nation
Musqueam Nation
Nanaimo First Nation
Nat'oot'en First Nation (Lake Babine)
Nazko Indian Band
Nuu'Chah'Nulth Tribal Council
Oweekeno Nation
Pavillion Indian Band
Quatsino Nation
Sechelt Indian Band
Sliammon Indian Band
Squamish Nation
Tahltan Tribal Council
Taku River Tlingit First Nation
Te-Mexw Treaty Association
Teslin Tlingit First Nation
Treaty Eight Tribal Association
Tsawwassen First Nation
Tsay-Key Dene Band
Tsimshian Nation
Tsleil-Waututh Nation (Burrard)
Westbank
Wet'suwet'en
Xaxli'p (Fountain Band)
Yale First Nation
Yekooche

Source: British Columbia Treaty Commission

Appendix C: Chronology of Events Contributing to the Treaty-Making Process in British Columbia

1774
Royal Proclamation of 1763 proclaimed by King George III of England. It is a statement of British policy recognizing Indian lands and rights and prohibiting alienation of Indian land except by cession to the Crown. The Proclamation has never been repealed and has the force of law in Canada, recognized in section 25 of the Constitution Act of 1982.

Spanish explorers arrive on the West Coast of Vancouver Island.

1778
Captain Cook explores the coast of British Columbia, establishing a British claim to sovereignty in opposition to that made earlier by the Spanish.

1849
Vancouver Island declared a colony of Britain. Britain gives the Hudson's Bay Company a grant over the land and its settlement.

1850-4
Governor James Douglas negotiates fourteen treaties with aboriginal groups on Vancouver Island, covering approximately 358 square miles (576 square kilometres) of land. In these 'purchases' or 'deeds of conveyance,' land was exchanged for payments in the form of blankets and the rights to hunt and fish on unoccupied Crown lands. He attempts to set a policy of granting a minimum of ten acres per family for reserve land. These treaties represent some recognition of aboriginal rights.

1858
The Mainland of British Columbia declared a colony of Britain.

1864
Joseph Trutch, a surveyor and developer, is appointed commissioner of lands and works. Trutch denies aboriginal title and sets forth a policy of prohibiting rights of pre-emption to aboriginal people and adjusting the size of reserve land.

1866
The colonies of Vancouver Island and the Mainland of British Columbia are unified.

1867
The British North America Act of 1867 creates the Dominion of Canada. Sections 91-94 give the federal government overall responsibility for administering Indian affairs and maintaining British colonial policy. Section 109 gives jurisdiction and ownership of land and natural resources to the provincial governments.

1870
Rupert's Land and the Northwestern Territory are transferred to Canada by Britain after the termination of the charter of the Hudson's Bay Company. Canada accepts responsibility for settling Indian claims in the area.

1871
British Columbia enters the Canadian federation.

Joseph Trutch is appointed lieutenant-governor of British Columbia.

1871-7
Treaties One to Seven are signed on the prairie provinces. Following the practice established in these treaties, British Columbia Natives hope that with Confederation the federal government will grant reserves in British Columbia on the basis of 160 acres (65 hectares) or more per family.

1876
The federal government passes the Indian Act, thus consolidating all federal legislation affecting aboriginal people. Indian status is defined, and the superintendent general is given sweeping administrative powers over many aspects of Indian life.

1881
A delegation of Nisga'a travels to Victoria demanding additional reserve land. Several years later a delegation of Tsimshian travels to Ottawa. They meet with Prime Minister Macdonald, who gives the chiefs his reassurance that the issue of insufficient reserve land will be addressed.

1884
The potlatch is made illegal through an amendment to the Indian Act. The amendment reads: 'Every Indian or other person who engages in or assists in celebrating the Indian festival known as the potlatch ... is guilty of a misdemeanour and shall be liable to imprisonment for a term of no more than six months and no less than two months.'

1890
The Nisga'a Land Committee is formally organized by Arthur Calder.

1899
Treaty Eight is signed with the Beaver, Cree, and Slave Indians located in the Peace River District of the province.

1906
A delegation from Squamish travels to England with a petition for treaties.

1909
Twenty tribes from southern British Columbia send delegates to London.

1912
A Memorandum of Agreement is signed by special commissioner J.A.J. McKenna and Premier Sir Richard McBride, appointing a commission to 'adjust' the acreage of Indian reserves in British Columbia.

1913
The Nisga'a petition to the British Privy Council, demanding a legal judgment on their land claim, is formally adopted by the Nisga'a Land Commission. It is the first aboriginal group to assert a legal right to land based upon the Royal Proclamation of 1763.

1916
The Allied Tribes of British Columbia (ATBC) is formed, comprising aboriginal groups from the coast and the interior of the province. A.E. O'Meara is retained as counsel by the ATBC. He pursues the land issues for his clients on a number of legal points until such activity is prohibited by law in 1927.

The McKenna-McBride Commission releases to the federal and provincial governments a report of its findings in relation to Indian reserves in British Columbia. Some existing reserves are confirmed as previously allotted, others reduced in size, and others eliminated because they are considered to be 'no longer required for Indian use and occupancy.' The commission's recommendations were not accepted by the provincial and federal government until 1920.

1921

Indian Agent Halliday, supported by federal commissioner Duncan Campbell Scott, prosecutes and imprisons Kwakiutl Indians participating in a potlatch. Masks, coppers, blankets, and other ceremonial regalia are confiscated.

1927

Joint parliamentary committee in Ottawa finds that land claims have no legal basis. The committee also recommends a prohibition on the raising of money for land claims. The recommendation is later codified in section 141 of the Indian Act.

1931

The Native Brotherhood of British Columbia (NBBC) is formed in the wake of the ATBC.

1938

British Columbia Order in Council 1036 gives final conveyance of title to Indian reserves in British Columbia to the federal government.

1949

British Columbia Indians receive the right to vote in provincial elections. Frank Calder elected to the provincial legislature.

1951

The Indian Act is amended, and laws prohibiting the potlatch and land claim activities are repealed.

1960

Conservative government of John Diefenbaker gives aboriginal people the right to vote in federal elections.

1969

Ottawa introduces the White Paper, which seeks to eliminate certain 'privileges' of aboriginal people, by abolishing the Indian Act and federal obligations to aboriginal people. The White Paper is condemned by many aboriginal groups in Canada as a form of cultural genocide.

Nisga'a Tribal Council launches legal action against the Crown in right of the Province of British Columbia, arguing that, in the absence of a treaty with the Crown, it still holds aboriginal title to its ancestral lands in the Nass Valley.

1971

Ottawa establishes the Core Funding Program for aboriginal groups, providing them with the necessary resources to promote their claims through research, legal action, and publicity.

1973

Supreme Court of Canada rules in *Calder*. Six justices find that the Nisga'a held aboriginal title before the assertion of British sovereignty. Three justices rule that aboriginal title continues to exist in the province; three justices rule that aboriginal title had been extinguished by the assertion of British sovereignty and, implicitly, by colonial actions prior to

1871. The appeal is ultimately dismissed, since the Nisga'a failed to obtain a fiat from the British Columbia government to launch the action. However, the divided ruling of the Court on aboriginal title in British Columbia induces the federal government to adopt a new policy on aboriginal people. Ottawa later enters into negotiations with the Nisga'a.

1977
Gitxsan-Wet'suwet'en Tribal Council begins research on their land claim.

1981
Federal government outlines a new comprehensive claims procedure in a publication entitled *In All Fairness*. Ottawa accepts only six claims nationally and one in British Columbia. The Nisga'a claim is formally accepted for negotiation.

1982
Ottawa outlines new policy on specific claims in the publication entitled *Outstanding Business*.

Patriation of the Canadian Constitution. The British North America Act of 1867 is amended and renamed the Constitution Act of 1867. New provisions are added in the Constitution Act of 1982; the Charter of Rights and Freedoms is also proclaimed into force on April 17. The Constitution Act of 1982 contains the following provisions in relation to aboriginal people:

Section 25
The guarantee in this Charter of certain rights and freedoms shall not be construed so as to abrogate or derogate from any aboriginal, treaty or other rights or freedoms that pertain to the aboriginal peoples of Canada, including:
a.) any rights or freedoms that have been recognized by the Royal Proclamation of October 7, 1763; and
b.) any rights or freedoms that now exist by way of land claims settlement.

Section 35
1. The existing aboriginal and treaty rights of the aboriginal peoples of Canada are hereby recognized and affirmed.
2. In this Act, 'aboriginal peoples of Canada' includes the Indian, Inuit and Metis peoples of Canada.
3. For greater certainty, in subsection (1) 'treaty rights' includes rights that now exist by way of land claims agreements or may be so acquired.
4. Notwithstanding any other provision of this Act, the aboriginal and treaty rights referred to in subsection (1) are guaranteed equally to male and female persons.

Section 37
1. A constitutional conference composed of the Prime Minister of Canada and the first ministers of the provinces shall be convened by the Prime Minister of Canada within one year after this Part comes into force.
2. The conference convened under subsection (1) shall have included in its agenda an item respecting constitutional matters that directly affect the aboriginal peoples of Canada, including the identification and definition of the rights of those peoples to be included in the Constitution of Canada, and the Prime Minister of Canada shall invite representatives of those peoples to participate in the discussions on that item.

The first section 37 conference to define aboriginal rights is held. The first ministers meet with aboriginal leaders.

1983
The Special Committee on Indian Self-Government in Canada tables its report (known as the Penner Report) and recommends that the federal government 'establish a new relationship with First Nations and that an essential element of this relationship be recognition of Indian Self-Government'; this relationship is to be 'explicitly stated and entrenched in the Constitution of Canada.'

1984
Federal government under Prime Minister Trudeau proposes constitutional entrenchment of aboriginal self-government by way of a constitutional accord at the second section 37 conference. Western provinces reject the proposal.

1985
Bill C-31 enacted by Parliament, restoring status and band membership to Native women, lost under section 12(1)(b) of the Indian Act. The bill also restores status to their children but does not give the children band membership.

Nuu'Chah'Nulth Tribal Council applies to the British Columbia Supreme Court for an injunction to prevent logging on Meares Island until the question of aboriginal title is settled. Justice Gibbs rules that aboriginal title does not apply to British Columbia. Decision appealed to the British Columbia Appeal Court, which gives the tribal council until September of 1986 to prepare their case.

British Columbia Court of Appeal in *Martin* grants injunction to the Nuu'Chah'Nulth Tribal Council. Court expresses the opinion that the nature and scope of aboriginal title should be negotiated and not decided by litigation.

1986
Bill C-93, the Sechelt Indian Band Self-Government Act, is enacted by Parliament. The Act gives the Sechelt 'municipal style' powers of self-government.

Federal Task Force established to review Ottawa's comprehensive claims policy releases its report entitled *Living Treaties, Lasting Agreements*. The report recommends affirmation by the federal government of aboriginal title and suggests that comprehensive claim negotiations need no longer be based on the extinguishment or surrender of aboriginal title.

1987
Gitxsan and Wet'suwet'en tribal nations launch a legal action in the British Columbia Supreme Court, claiming a right of ownership and jurisdiction to their ancestral lands. The case is known as *Delgamuukw*.

1988
Social Credit government in British Columbia creates its first Ministry of Native Affairs. Jack Weisgerber is the minister. The government still refuses to recognize aboriginal title in the province.

1990
Meech Lake Accord is defeated due to the failure of the Manitoba and Newfoundland legislatures to pass companion legislation.

Quebec police raid a Mohawk road barricade erected at Oka to block the expansion of a golf course onto Mohawk land. At the nearby Kahnawake reserve, Mohawks block the Mercier bridge, cutting off a major artery of Montreal. The Oka standoff becomes a symbol to aboriginal people across Canada of the failure of government to resolve land claims.

Other blockades are set up throughout Canada, with some in British Columbia. Premier Vander Zalm visits some of these blockades and addresses the protesters. By the fall of 1990, Vander Zalm announces that his government will commence negotiations with First Nations.

British Columbia Claims Task Force established.

1991
British Columbia Claims Task Force releases its report. The task force recommends a six-stage treaty negotiation process and the formation of the British Columbia Treaty Commission to facilitate negotiations.

British Columbia Supreme Court rules in *Delgamuukw*, rejecting the tribal nations' claim. Chief Justice McEachern finds that aboriginal title had been extinguished in British Columbia. The Gitxsan and Wet'suwet'en seek leave to appeal to the British Columbia Court of Appeal.

1992
Representatives of the First Nations Summit and the federal and British Columbia governments make a formal commitment to negotiate treaties in British Columbia by signing the British Columbia Treaty Commission Agreement.

Charlottetown Accord is defeated in a national referendum. The Accord contained a provision recognizing aboriginal self-government.

1993
British Columbia Treaty Commission is appointed to function as an independent and impartial tripartite body to assist in the facilitation of treaty negotiations in British Columbia. By December, a number of First Nations indicate their desire to negotiate a treaty.

In June, the British Columbia Court of Appeal rules in *Delgamuukw*. The Court rules that not all aboriginal rights of the Gitxsan and Wet'suwet'en tribal nations were extinguished in 1871. Those that remain, however, do not entail the unfettered right to use, occupy, and control the lands and resources of the area. The Court also emphasizes that determining the nature and scope of these aboriginal rights and the type of self-government that the Gitxsan and Wet'suwet'en shall enjoy, outside the Indian Act, should be done through negotiation.

1995
A number of Native blockades are established in the interior of the province to protest the impact of commercial development on nearby reserve land. A standoff erupts at Gustafsen Lake. The 'Defenders of the Shuswap Nation' protest the non-Native occupation of their land in the absence of treaties. The blockade is eventually dismantled by the RCMP.

1996
The Nisga'a Agreement in Principle is initialled and signed by representatives of the Nisga'a Tribal Council and the federal and British Columbia governments.

Notes

Introduction

1 R. Fisher, *Contact and Conflict: Indian-European Relations in British Columbia, 1774-1890* (Vancouver: UBC Press 1977).
2 F. Cassidy and N. Dale, *After Native Claims? The Implications of Comprehensive Claims Settlements for Natural Resources in British Columbia* (Halifax: Institute for Research on Public Policy 1988).
3 P. Tennant, *Aboriginal Peoples and Politics: The Indian Land Question in British Columbia, 1849-1989* (Vancouver: UBC Press 1990).
4 M. Smith, *Our Home or Native Land?* (Victoria: Crown Western 1995).

Chapter 1: Prelude to the Treaty-Making Process

1 H.W. Hertzberg, *The Search for an American Indian Identity* (Syracuse, NY: Syracuse University Press 1971), 1.
2 In the American context see H.F. Dobins, 'Native American Population Collapse and Recovery,' in W.R. Swagerty, ed., *Scholars and the Indian Experience: Critical Reviews of Recent Writing in the Social Sciences* (Bloomington, IN: Indiana University Press 1984), 28-9. Note that underestimating indigenous populations intentionally seems to have been rather widespread, extending to most areas subject to the colonizing efforts of European powers. For a consideration of the demographic studies of several Pacific Island states, see A.F. Bushnell, ' "The Horror" Reconsidered: An Evaluation of the Historical Evidence for Population Decline in Hawai'i, 1778-1803,' *Pacific Studies* 16, no. 3 (1993): 115.
3 R.C. Downes, 'A Crusade for Indian Reform, 1922-1934,' *Mississippi Valley Historical Review* 32, no. 2 (1942): 342.
4 Canada, Department of Indian Affairs and Northern Development, *Indian Register Population by Sex and Residence: 1993*, March 1994, xv.
5 S. Cornell, *The Return of the Native: American Indian Political Resurgence* (Toronto: University of Toronto Press 1988), 57.
6 I am indebted to Professor Paul Tennant for much of the content of this section of this chapter. See Tennant, *Aboriginal Peoples and Politics*, 6-9.
7 See Judson in *Calder* v. *Attorney General of British Columbia* (1973), 34 *Dominion Law Reports* (3d), 328.
8 The common law comprises the body of principles and rules of action affecting government, people, and property which derive their authority either from long-standing customs or from the judgments of courts recognizing and enforcing such customs. *Black's Law Dictionary*, 5th ed. (St. Paul, MN: West Publishing Company 1979), 250-1.
9 B. Slattery, 'The Hidden Constitution: Aboriginal Rights in Canada,' in M. Boldt and

J.A. Long, eds., *The Quest for Justice: Aboriginal People and Aboriginal Rights* (Toronto: University of Toronto Press 1985), 118. It is important to note that the law in British Columbia is unsettled as regards the doctrine of continuity. In the 1993 *Delgamuukw* case, the doctrine of continuity was acknowledged by Lambert in his dissenting opinion, whereas one of the judges for the Court's majority, Wallace, rejected it.

10 For a fuller explanation see D. Sanders, 'Getting Back to Rights,' in F. Cassidy, ed., *Aboriginal Title in British Columbia: Delgamuukw v. The Queen* (Montreal: Institute for Research on Public Policy 1992), 285.

11 *Bear Island Foundation* v. *Attorney General of Ontario* (1991), 83 *Dominion Law Reports* (4th), 381-4.

12 *Delgamuukw* v. *The Queen* (1993), 104 *Dominion Law Reports* (4th), 537. See also *R. v. Sparrow* (1990), 70 *Dominion Law Reports* (4th), 408.

13 B.H. Kellock and F.C.M. Anderson, 'A Theory of Aboriginal Rights,' in F. Cassidy, ed., *Aboriginal Title in British Columbia*, 102.

14 *Delgamuukw*, 537.

15 D.W. Elliott, ed., *Law and Aboriginal Peoples of Canada*, 2nd ed. (North York, ON: Captus Press 1992), 75.

16 See, for example, the *Treaty of Peace between the Iroquois and the Governor de Tracy*, New York Papers 111 A28. The text of the treaty can be found in C. Parry, ed., *The Consolidated Treaty Series*, vol. 9 (Dobbs Ferry: Oceana, 1969-1986), 363.

17 However, it should be noted that not all of the treaties concluded at this time were designed to ensure peace between the French and aboriginal people. The relationship between these powers was often fluid, and sometimes difficult to define. Therefore the provisions of the treaties varied, with some intended to settle conflicts, and others designed to acquire land. See P. Cumming and A. Mickenberg, eds., *Native Rights in Canada*, 2nd ed. (Toronto: General 1974), 295.

18 See for example the James Bay Agreement of 1975, the Northeastern Quebec Agreement of 1978, the Inuvialuit Agreement of 1984, and the Nunavut Agreement of 1993.

19 See *Guerin* v. *The Queen*, [1984] 2 *Supreme Court Reports*, 335.

20 For a review see B. Slattery, 'The Land Rights of Indigenous Canadian Peoples' (Ph.D. diss., University of Saskatchewan 1970), 350.

21 B. Ryder, 'The Demise and Rise of the Classical Paradigm in Canadian Federalism: Promoting the Autonomy of the Provinces and First Nations,' *McGill Law Journal* 36 (1991): 308.

22 For a discussion of the obligation to pay compensation for extinguishment of aboriginal title, see B. Slattery, 'Understanding Aboriginal Rights,' *Canadian Bar Review* 66 (1987): 751.

23 See the dissenting view of the Court in *St. Catharines Milling Co.* v. *R.*, [1887] 13 *Supreme Court Reports*, 608.

24 *Mitchell* v. *United States*, 34 *United States Reports* 711 (1835), 746

25 *R.* v. *Sioui*, [1990] 3 *Canadian Native Law Reporter*, 127.

26 A. Fleras and J.E. Elliott, *The Nations Within: Aboriginal-State Relations in Canada, the United States, and New Zealand* (Toronto: Oxford University Press 1992), 23.

27 Ibid.

28 Ibid., 24-6.

29 Fisher, *Contact and Conflict*, 42.

30 Tennant, *Aboriginal Peoples and Politics*, 17.

31 Letter from A. Barclay, Secretary, Hudson's Bay Company, to J. Douglas, December 1849; cited in D. Pethick, *James Douglas: Servant of Two Empires* (Vancouver: Mitchell Press 1969), 77-8.

32 See letter from J. Douglas to A. Barclay, 3 September 1849, Public Archives of Canada, A-11/72.

33 Smith, *Our Home or Native Land?* 76.

34 Tennant, *Aboriginal Peoples and Politics*, 20.

35 For a review of British treaties with indigenous peoples similar to the Treaty of Waitangi of 1840, see D.V. Williams, 'Te Tiriti o Waitangi – Unique Relationship Between the Crown and Tangata Whenua,' in I.H. Kawharu, ed., *Waitangi: Maori and Pakeha Perspectives of the Treaty of Waitangi* (Auckland: Oxford University Press 1989), 64.

36 K. Puri, 'Copyright Protection for Australian Aborigines in the Light of Mabo,' in M.A. Stephenson and S. Ratnapala, eds., *Mabo: A Judicial Revolution* (St. Lucia, Queensland: University of Queensland Press 1993), 147.

37 Incidentally, this form of acquisition was used often by the British in respect of other colonies, especially New Zealand and the Pacific Island states of Samoa and Fiji. One should note, however, that in the case of Fiji, the island was ceded to the British Crown on a less than voluntary basis, as a response to a threat of a military invasion by the United States. For an account see M. Twain, *Following the Equator: A Journey Around the World*, vol. 1 (Hopewell, NJ: Ecco Press 1992), 35.

38 Letter from Lord Carnavon to Douglas, 11 April 1858; cited in British Columbia, *Papers Connected with the Indian Land Question, 1858-1875* (Victoria: Queen's Printer 1875), 18.

39 W. Duff, 'The Fort Victoria Treaties,' *BC Studies* 3 (1969): 6.

40 Cited in Tennant, *Aboriginal Peoples and Politics*, 21-2.

41 To offer some examples: the editor of the *British Colonist* insisted that 'nothing but negligence [on the part of colonial and Imperial authorities] has prevented the extinction of Indian title long ago'; while others referred to the continuation of such rights as a 'bugbear to stop settlement.' See Tennant, *Aboriginal People and Politics*, 23.

42 For an account of the colonial efforts of the British in the South Pacific generally, and the actions of the London Missionary Society in particular, see A. Moorehead, *The Fatal Impact: An Account of the Invasion of the South Pacific, 1767-1840* (Honolulu: Mutual Publishing 1966), 79-85.

43 See letter from J. Douglas to Duke of Newcastle, 18 October 1859; cited in Fisher, *Contact and Conflict*, 150.

44 Tennant, *Aboriginal Peoples and Politics*, 30.

45 Ibid., 31.

46 See letter from R.M. Parsons to Sapper Turnbull, 1 May 1861, in *Papers Connected with the Indian Land Question in British Columbia*, 22.

47 W. Duff, *The Indian History of British Columbia*, vol. 1, *The Impact of the White Man* (Victoria: Provincial Museum of British Columbia 1965), 61.

48 Fisher, *Contact and Conflict*, 153.

49 As Fisher has noted: 'British Columbia and Vancouver Island were never among the most crucial concerns of the Imperial authorities, and other colonies demanded, and got, more attention.' See *Contact and Conflict*, 159.

50 Ibid., 158-9.

51 P. Tennant, 'Aboriginal Peoples and Aboriginal Title in British Columbia Politics,' in R. K. Carty, ed., *British Columbia Government and Politics* (Vancouver: UBC Press 1996).

52 See *Papers Connected with the Indian Land Question in British Columbia*, section titled 'Report on Indian Reserves,' Appendix B, 11.

53 Tennant, *Aboriginal Peoples and Politics*, 40.

54 Ibid.

55 Ibid.

56 Ibid.

57 A member of the New Zealand Company offered the following remarks in respect of the treaties signed between the Maori and the British Crown: 'We have always had serious doubts whether the Treaty of Waitangi, made with naked savages by a counsel invested with no plenipotentiary powers, without ratification by the Crown, could be treated by lawyers as anything but a praiseworthy device for amusing and pacifying savages for the moment.' See Letter from J. Somes, Governor of New Zealand Company, to Colonial Secretary, 1843; cited in R. Macdonald, *The Maori of New Zealand* (London: Expedite Graphic 1985), 8

58 Tennant, *Aboriginal Peoples and Politics*, 41.
59 Ibid., 43.
60 British Columbia, *British North America Act, 1867, Terms of Union with Canada, Rules and Orders of the Legislative Assembly* . . . (Victoria: R. Wolfenden 1881), 66; cited in Fisher, *Contact and Conflict*, 177.
61 Tennant, *Aboriginal Peoples and Politics*, 44.
62 Fisher, *Contact and Conflict*, 177.
63 See sections 55 to 57 and section 90 of the Constitution Act of 1867.
64 See letter from L.W. Herchmer, Commissioner of the North West Mounted Police, to the Controller, North West Mounted Police, 2 December 1897, Public Archives of Canada, RG 10, Black Series, vol. 3848, file 75, 236-1.
65 Cited in C. Mair, *Through the Mackenzie Basin: A Narrative of the Athabasca and Peace River Expedition of 1899* (Toronto: University of Toronto Press 1908), 23-4.
66 See letter from A.E. Forget, Indian Commissioner of the Northwest Territories, to J.A. McKenna, Department of Indian Affairs, *Ottawa Citizen*, 28 June 1898.
67 See letter from H.A. Conroy, Inspector for Treaty 8, to Superintendent of Indian Affairs, 29 October 1910, Public Archives of Canada, RG 10, Black Series, vol. 1, file 1/1-11-5-11.
68 D. Madill, *British Columbia Indian Treaties in Historical Perspective* (Ottawa: Research Branch, Indian and Northern Affairs Canada 1981), 51.
69 R. Daniel, 'The Spirit and Terms of Treaty Eight,' in R. Price, ed., *The Spirit of the Alberta Indian Treaties* (Montreal: Institute for Research on Public Policy 1980), 80.
70 This was a problem associated with many of the numbered treaties concluded in the Canadian West. For a detailed examination in the context of the Stoney Indians of Alberta, see I.A.L. Getty and J.W. Warner, *The Kootenay Plains and the Bighorn Wesley Stoney Band: An Oral and Documentary Historical Study, 1800-1970* (Morley, AB: Stoney Tribal Administration Band Council, 1972).
71 Tennant, *Aboriginal Peoples and Politics*, 66
72 Ibid., 55.
73 Ibid.
74 Ibid., 58.
75 The reduction (or 'cut-offs') of aboriginal reserve land was codified in the British Columbia Lands Settlement Act of 1920. The legislation was enacted pursuant to some of the recommendations of the McKenna-McBride Commission Report of 1916, empowered to 'settle all differences between the Governments of the Dominion and the Province respecting Indian lands and Indian affairs,' and to offer a 'final adjustment of all matters relating to Indian Affairs in the Province.' See British Columbia, Royal Commission on Indian Affairs in the Province of British Columbia, *Evidence* (Victoria: Acme Press 1916). The McKenna-McBride Commission did not, however, consider treaties and self-government.
76 Note that the Judicial Committee of the Privy Council was the final appellate court for claims arising in Canada (and indeed in other British colonies) until 1949, after which the Supreme Court of Canada assumed this function. The Judicial Committee case arising from Nigeria is cited as *Amodu Tijani* v. *Secretary, Southern Nigeria* (1921), 2 Appeal Court, 409-410.
77 Tennant, *Aboriginal Peoples and Politics*, 114-19.
78 For an in-depth overview and analysis of the major aboriginal political organizations in British Columbia from the late 1950s to the late 1980s, see Tennant, *Aboriginal Peoples and Politics*, chapters 10, 12, 13, and 14.
79 *Calder* v. *Attorney General of British Columbia*, [1973] *Supreme Court Reports*, 313.
80 Fleras and Elliott, *The Nations Within: Aboriginal-State Relations in Canada, the United States, and New Zealand*, 44-5.
81 Ibid.
82 See *Guerin*, 335.
83 *Martin et al.*, v. *The Queen in Right of the Province of British Columbia, et al.*, [1985] 3 *Western Weekly Reports*, 583-593 (B.C.C.A.).

84 Ibid., 607.
85 Tennant, *Aboriginal Peoples and Politics*, 218-25.
86 See 'B.C. Native Bands Take to the Barricades to Push Their Cause,' *Maclean's*, 7 August 1995, 10.
87 Tennant, *Aboriginal Peoples and Politics*, 236-7.
88 The blockades in British Columbia were focussed primarily on the absence of treaties in the province; in Alberta, where there are treaties with First Nations, the blockade near the Oldman River dam by the Peigan First Nation, for example, focussed on Treaty 7 promises allegedly left unfulfilled by the federal government.
89 A analysis of the *Delgamuukw* case is found in P.T. Burns, 'Delgamuukw: A Summary of the Judgment,' in F. Cassidy, ed., *Aboriginal Title in British Columbia*, 21.
90 Leave was granted to appeal the decision to the Supreme Court of Canada on 10 February 1994.
91 *Delgamuukw v. The Queen in Right of the Province of British Columbia and the Attorney General of Canada*, Vancouver Registry CA 013770, 25 June 1993, 73.
92 Ibid.

Chapter 2: The Process of Treaty-Making

1 *Report of the British Columbia Claims Task Force*, 28 June 1991, 74-5.
2 See Appendix 1 for a complete list of the task force's recommendations.
3 See *Agreement Between the First Nations Summit and Her Majesty the Queen in Right of Canada and Her Majesty the Queen in Right of the Province of British Columbia*, 21 September 1992.
4 Ibid., 5-9.
5 See *Memorandum of Understanding Between Canada and British Columbia Respecting the Sharing of Pre-Treaty Costs, Settlement Costs, Implementation Costs, and the Costs of Self-Government*, 21 June 1993.
6 Ibid., 2-3.
7 Ibid., 3.
8 Ibid., 4.
9 Ibid., 4-5.
10 Ibid., 5.
11 Ibid., 6.
12 Ibid., 6-7.
13 Ibid., 7.
14 Ibid., 8.
15 See 'True Self-Government vs. The Canadian Government's Proposal for Indian Self-Government,' *Kahtou*, 15 May 1994.
16 It should be noted that the UBCIC has established an ongoing government-to-government relationship with Victoria, in order to resolve a series of policy concerns of mutual interest. Yet the UBCIC has made it clear that such interaction and cooperation does not derogate from the bilateral nation-to-nation relationship between First Nations and the federal government. See *Memorandum of Understanding Respecting the Establishment of a Government-to-Government Relationship Between the Union of B.C. Indian Chiefs and the Government of British Columbia*, 11 June 1993.
17 British Columbia, News Release, 19 September 1993. See also *Protocol Between the Province of British Columbia and the Union of BC Municipalities for Implementing the Memorandum of Understanding on Local Government Participation in Aboriginal Treaty Negotiations*, 22 March 1993.
18 See British Columbia, 'Instructions on Open Negotiations,' 19 September 1994.
19 *Protocol Respecting the Government-to-Government Relationship Between the First Nations Summit and the Government of British Columbia*, 20 August 1993, 2-3.
20 British Columbia, *British Columbia's Approach to Interim Measures Regarding Lands and Resources*, 30 May 1995, 8-11.

21 Ibid., 12-15.
22 A. Pape, 'Interim Measures in the B.C. Context,' paper presented at the Interim Measures During Treaty Negotiations Workshop, Pacific Business and Law Institute, 22 April 1994, Vancouver, BC, 6-7.
23 See section entitled 'Limitations' in British Columbia, *British Columbia's Approach to Interim Measures Regarding Lands and Resources* (Draft), 25 April 1995.

Chapter 3: The Issues to Be Negotiated
1 See 'Urban Crowding Complicates Native Land Claims,' *Vancouver Sun*, 15 December 1994, B2.
2 J.P. Taylor and G. Paget, 'Federal/Provincial Responsibility and the Sechelt,' in D. Hawkes, ed., *Aboriginal Peoples and Government Responsibility: Exploring Federal and Provincial Roles* (Ottawa: Carleton University Press 1991), 303-5.
3 D. Hawkes, 'Introduction,' in Ibid., 14-15.
4 Note that as of September of 1995, the District of Sechelt announced it will hold public hearings for all to attend to discuss the contents of the proposed Agreement in Principle.
5 Tom Paul, Land Claims Negotiator with Sechelt, interview with the author, 29 August 1995. See 'The Alleged Indian Outrage at Jervis Inlet,' *Mainland Guardian*, 24 December 1874.
6 'Sechelt Land Claim,' position paper prepared by the Sechelt Indian Band, February 1995, 1-5.
7 Ibid., 2.
8 Ibid., 3-4.
9 See *Records of Decisions and Commitments* by Sechelt, Canada, and British Columbia, 15 July 1995.
10 Ibid., 3.
11 Ibid., 5.
12 Tom Paul, Land Claims Negotiator with Sechelt, interview with the author, 22 August 1995.
13 *Nuu'Chah'Nulth Ha'Wiih Position on Lands, Waters, Air, and Natural Resources*, no date, 3. Hereinafter referred to as *Nuu'Chah'Nulth Position*.
14 *Nuu'Chah'Nulth Position*, 3.
15 Ibid.
16 Ibid., 6.
17 Ibid., 4.
18 Ibid., 6. Note that there appears to be some international precedent for this position. The International Whaling Commission, despite a 1986 worldwide moratorium imposed on all commercial whaling, allows aboriginal peoples to harvest whales in perpetuity, at levels appropriate to their cultural and nutritional requirements.
19 Ibid., 9.
20 Ibid., 10.
21 Ibid., 11.
22 See *Accord of Recognition and Respect*, 13 June 1994.
23 Chief Don Ryan, interview with the author, 30 August 1995.
24 One should note that the authority of the Gitxsan hereditary chiefs over fisheries in traditional tribal territory has been long-standing, but it has also been a sore point in their relations with Ottawa.
25 Chief Don Ryan, interview with the author, 30 August 1995.
26 Ibid.
27 Chief Elmer Derrick, interview with the author, 6 October 1995.
28 Chief Elmer Derrick, interview with the author, 8 March 1996.
29 Prior to the formal signing of the Nisga'a Agreement in Principle, a number of forestry companies and umbrella organizations took out a full-page advertisement in the *Vancouver Sun,* indicating their opposition to the agreement on the basis that they had not received a sufficient amount of time to respond to its provisions.

30 Canada, Federal Treaty Negotiations Office (Vancouver), *British Columbia Treaty Negotiations: The Federal Perspective* (Draft), 27 June 1995, 14. Hereinafter referred to as *The Federal Perspective*.
31 British Columbia, *British Columbia's Approach to Treaty Settlements, Lands, and Resources*, 12 May 1995, 3-4. Hereinafter referred to as *B.C.'s Approach*.
32 Ibid., 12.
33 *The Federal Perspective*, 15.
34 In New Zealand, for example, the government recently paid $6.85 million to buy out a number of pastoral leases in the Greenstone Valley as part of a possible land claim settlement with the Ngai Tahu.
35 *B.C.'s Approach*, 5.
36 *The Federal Perspective*, 15.
37 *B.C.'s Approach*, 7
38 *The Federal Perspective*, 17.
39 Ibid., 17-18.
40 See the decision of Justice Lambert of the British Columbia Court of Appeal in *Dick* v. *R.*, [1986] 1 *Western Weekly Reports*, 11.
41 *The Federal Perspective*, 18.
42 Ibid., 18-20
43 Ibid., 21-3.
44 Ibid., 23-4.
45 See 'Natives Offered Limited Powers,' *Globe and Mail*, 11 August 1995, A1.
46 *The Federal Perspective*, 24.
47 Ibid.
48 Ibid.

Chapter 4: The Treaty-Making Process Considered

1 *Report of the British Columbia Claims Task Force*, 55.
2 Letter from members of TNAC to the Honourable Ron Irwin, minister of Indian affairs and northern development, and to the Honourable John Cashore, minister of aboriginal affairs, 29 September 1994.
3 See V. Palmer, 'Third Parties Blast Land-Claims Secrecy,' *Vancouver Sun*, 30 September 1994.
4 Canada, Department of Indian and Northern Affairs, Communiqué, 30 September 1994.
5 'Municipalities to Get Front-Row Seating at Indian Treaty Talks,' *Vancouver Sun*, 24 September 1994, B1.
6 V. Palmer, ' "Land Claims Process Chaos," Says Forestry Industry,' *Vancouver Sun*, 31 March 1995, A18.
7 'Minister Pleads for Fairness in Aboriginal Treaty Talks,' *Vancouver Sun*, 3 May 1994, B2.
8 'Native Bands Opting for Public Land-Claims Talks,' *Vancouver Sun*, 3 May 1994, B2. It should be noted that in the case of the Sechelt band, notwithstanding their efforts to open up their negotiations to the public, and the media's criticism of a 'closed door' process, the negotiations have been largely unattended by the public, with only a handful of people sitting in on the sessions.
9 'Land-Claims Talks to Be Open to the Public,' *Vancouver Sun*, 3 March 1995, C10.
10 V. Palmer, 'Third Party in Aboriginal Talks Finds It's Not Invited,' *Vancouver Sun*, 27 March 1995, A10.
11 Mike Hunter, president of the Fisheries Council of British Columbia, interview with the author, 20 July 1995.
12 COFI, *Council of Forest Industries Response to British Columbia's Discussion Papers*, August 1995, 19.
13 B.C. Chamber of Commerce, *Policy on Aboriginal Land Claims*, 42.
14 Interview with the author, 4 August 1995.
15 See '$8 Billion Owed in Unsettled Land Claims,' *Vancouver Sun*, 24 October 1994, A7.

16 See J. Hume, 'Hush-Hush Land Claim Costs May Spook the Taxpayers,' *Times-Colonist*, 21 January 1995, A5.

17 According to Melvin Smith, $15 billion is a figure arrived at by a 'provincial insider, who [did] not wish to be named.' See M. Smith, *Our Home or Native Land?* 98.

18 'Land Claims, Mine Payoff, Cost Taxpayers $134 Million,' *Vancouver Sun*, 19 August 1995, A1.

19 The content of the Price Waterhouse study was articulated by former Indian affairs minister Tom Siddon when speaking to the Asia Pacific Institute Conference on 'The New Aboriginal Claims Settlement Process,' 5 February 1993, Vancouver, British Columbia.

20 KPMG, *Benefits and Costs of Treaty Settlements in British Columbia: A Financial and Economic Perspective*, Project Report (Victoria: 17 January 1996).

21 Ibid., 3.

22 Ibid., 5.

23 Ibid., 6.

24 Ibid., 7.

25 Ibid., 21.

26 For a review of this study, see 'Land Claims Study Released,' *Native Issues Monthly*, February 1996, 13.

27 Ibid.

28 Ibid.

29 Ibid.

30 See 'Ottawa Questions B.C.'s Desire to Negotiate,' *Vancouver Sun*, 15 July 1995, A7.

31 In addition to the costs associated with implementing the Nisga'a settlement, the cost of the negotiations totaled $3 million. See 'Obtaining Nisga'a Deal Cost B.C. $3 Million,' *Vancouver Sun*, 26 March 1996, B1.

32 *Nisga'a Treaty Negotiations Agreement in Principle*, 15 February 1996, section 2 (General Provisions). Hereinafter referred to as the *AIP*.

33 V. Palmer, 'Nisga'a Talks Indicate Land Claims to Cost Billions,' *Vancouver Sun*, 14 July 1995, A18.

34 *AIP*, section 1(a)(b) (Lands and Resources).

35 Ibid., section 16.

36 Ibid., section 93.

37 Ibid., section 19(a)(e) (Nisga'a Constitution).

38 Ibid., sections 11 and 12.

39 Ibid., section 22(a)(b) (Relations With Individuals Who Are Not Nisga'a Citizens).

40 Ibid., section 23.

41 Ibid., sections 27-74 (Nisga'a Government Legislative Jurisdiction And Authority).

42 Ibid., sections 2-18 (Police Services), and sections 26-43 (Nisga'a Court).

43 Ibid., section 9 (General Provisions).

44 Ibid., section 17(a)(b) (Salmon Harvest Entitlements).

45 Ibid., section 19.

46 Ibid., section 45 (Harvest Entitlements of Non-Salmon Species).

47 Ibid., section 62 (Fisheries Management).

48 Ibid., section 89 (Participation in the Coast-Wide Commercial Fishery).

49 Ibid., section 1 (Capital Transfer).

50 Ibid., section 2 (Fiscal Financing Agreements).

51 Ibid., section 5 (Nisga'a Lands), and section 1 (Nisga'a Nation Direct Taxation).

52 Ibid., section 6(a)(b)(c)(d) (Nisga'a Lands).

53 See 'Politics Cited as Indians See Harcourt Backing Off,' *Vancouver Sun*, 19 May 1995, B1. One should note that Victoria has indicated the total amount of land transferred will not exceed 5 per cent of the total land mass of the province, a figure that is arguably consistent with the population of aboriginal people as a percentage of the total population of British Columbia.

54 Smith, *Our Home or Native Land?*, 136.

55 Ibid., 134.
56 Ibid., 135.
57 Ibid.
58 Ibid.
59 Ibid, 135-6.
60 Ibid., 136.
61 The judgment of the Court's majority opinion is contained in D.W. Elliott, ed., *Law and Aboriginal Peoples in Canada*, 149-57.
62 Ibid., 157. One should note that the Court's recognition of aboriginal rights in traditional territories has had the impact of requiring an archaeological assessment of traditional land use before any area can be subject to a timber licence.
63 Ibid., 156.
64 Ibid., 157.
65 Smith, *Our Home or Native Land?* 141.
66 *Council of Forest Industries Response to British Columbia's Discussion Papers*, 10.
67 Ibid.
68 Ibid., 14.
69 Ibid.
70 Ibid., 14-15.
71 Reference here is to the Aboriginal Fisheries Strategy, which gives band councils management authority (formerly held by the federal Department of Fisheries and Oceans) over allowable catch levels. For a critique of the initiative, see Smith, *Our Home or Native Land?* 199-222.
72 Cited in Royal Commission on Aboriginal Peoples, *Treaty Making in the Spirit of Co-existence* (Ottawa: Minister of Supply and Services 1995), 46.
73 Cited in *Treaty Making in the Spirit of Co-existence*, 49.
74 Outside Canada, examples of treaties concluded with amending formulae are numerous, particularly between the United States and its former possessions in the South Pacific. A good example is the 1982 Compact of Association between the United States and the Federated States of Micronesia. For an overview see P. Larmour, 'The Federated States of Micronesia, Palau, Marshall Islands, and the Commonwealth of the Northern Marianas,' in P. Larmour and R. Qalo, eds., *Decentralization in the South Pacific: Local, Provincial and State Government in Twenty Countries* (Suva, Fiji: University of the South Pacific 1985), 337.
75 See M.S. Whittington, 'Aboriginal Self-Government in Canada,' in M.S. Whittington and G. Williams, eds., *Canadian Politics in the 1990s* (Toronto: Nelson Canada 1995), 16.

Chapter 5: The Future of Treaty-Making
1 See R. Dodson, 'First Nation Negotiations Better Than Courts and Confrontation,' *Vancouver Sun*, 20 July 1995, B3.
2 B. Clark, *Native Liberty, Crown Sovereignty: The Existing Right of Aboriginal Self-Government in Canada* (Montreal and Kingston: McGill-Queen's University Press 1990), 3.
3 'Bulletproof Vests Save Lives of Officers Caught in Ambush,' *Vancouver Sun*, 28 August 1995, A1.
4 'Indian Rebels Plan to "Leave in Body Bags," ' *Vancouver Sun*, 22 August 1995, A1.
5 'Indians' Case Doesn't Impress Legal Experts,' *Globe and Mail*, 31 August 1995, A4.
6 Ibid.
7 'Indians Ask Opposition Leaders How They'd Tackle Land Claims,' *Vancouver Sun*, 28 June 1995, B4.
8 Ibid.
9 For a review of the implications of using referenda, see P. Boyer, *The People's Mandate: Referendums and a More Democratic Canada* (Toronto: Dundurn Press 1992), 1-9.
10 Erling Christensen, chief negotiator for the Lheit-Lit'en and Yekooche First Nations, interview with author, 3 July 1996.

11 M. Boldt, *Surviving as Indians: The Challenge of Self-Government* (Toronto: University of Toronto Press 1993), 120.
12 Ibid., 121.
13 Ibid., 124-5.
14 Kimowanniwi Piyesiw, Letter to the Editor, *Globe and Mail*, 15 September 1995, A18.
15 See 'Indian Reservations: How to Succeed, How to Fail,' *The Economist*, 6-12 April 1996, 25-31.
16 Ibid., 25.
17 Ibid., 31.
18 *Council of Forest Industries Response to British Columbia's Discussion Papers*, 5.
19 Anonymous, interview with the author, 5 October 1995.
20 Ibid.
21 Ibid.
22 G. Knapp, *Native Timber Harvests in Southeast Alaska* (Portland: United States Department of Agriculture, Pacific Northwest Research Station, 1992).
23 Specific claims arise out of allegations of breaches of treaties or the Indian Act.
24 Indian Claims Commission, *Submission Guide* (Ottawa: Minister of Supply and Services, 1995).
25 Ibid., 10.
26 P. Temm, *The Waitangi Tribunal: The Conscience of the Nation* (Auckland: Random Century New Zealand 1990), 5.
27 G. Palmer, *New Zealand's Constitution in Crisis: Reforming Our Political System* (Dunedin: John McIndoe 1992), 78-82.
28 Ibid., 79. This was the case in the Te Atiawa claim of 1983. See *Report of the Waitangi Tribunal on the Motnui-Waitara Claim* (Wai-6, Government Printers, Wellington 1983).
29 G. Chapman, 'The Treaty of Waitangi – Fertile Ground for Judicial (and Academic) Myth-Making,' *New Zealand Law Journal* (1991): 235-6.
30 A. Chayes, 'The Role of the Judge in Public Law Litigation,' *Harvard Law Review* 89 (1976): 1282-3.
31 A.M. Bickel, *The Supreme Court and the Idea of Progress* (New York: Harper and Row 1970), 175.

Bibliography

Books, Articles, and Monographs

Bickel, A.M. *The Supreme Court and the Idea of Progress*. New York: Harper and Row 1970

Boldt, M. *Surviving as Indians: The Challenge of Self-Government*. Toronto: University of Toronto Press 1993

Boyer, P. *The People's Mandate: Referendums and a More Democratic Canada*. Toronto: Dundurn Press 1992

Cassidy, F., and N. Dale. *After Native Claims? The Implications of Comprehensive Claims Settlements for Natural Resources in British Columbia*. Halifax: Institute for Research on Public Policy 1988

Chapman, G. 'The Treaty of Waitangi – Fertile Ground for Judicial (and Academic) Myth-Making.' *New Zealand Law Journal* (1991): 235-6

Chayes, A. 'The Role of the Judge in Public Law Litigation.' *Harvard Law Review* 89 (1976): 1282-3

Clark, B. *Native Liberty, Crown Sovereignty: The Existing Right of Aboriginal Self-Government in Canada*. Montreal and Kingston: McGill-Queen's University Press 1990

Cornell, S. *The Return of the Native: American Indian Political Resurgence*. Toronto: University of Toronto Press 1988

Daniel, R. 'The Spirit and Terms of Treaty Eight.' In R. Price, ed., *The Spirit of the Alberta Indian Treaties*. Montreal: Institute for Research on Public Policy 1980

Downes, R.C. 'A Crusade for Indian Reform, 1922-1934.' *Mississippi Valley Historical Review* 32, no. 2 (1942): 342

Duff, W. 'The Fort Victoria Treaties.' *BC Studies* 3 (1969): 6

–. *The Indian History of British Columbia*. Vol. 1, *The Impact of the White Man*. Victoria: Provincial Museum of British Columbia 1965

Elliott, D.W., ed. *Law and Aboriginal Peoples of Canada*. 2nd ed. North York, ON: Captus Press 1992

Fisher, R. *Contact and Conflict: Indian-European Relations in British Columbia, 1774-1890*. Vancouver: UBC Press 1977

Fleras, A., and J.L. Elliott. *The Nations Within: Aboriginal-State Relations in Canada, the United States, and New Zealand*. Toronto: Oxford University Press 1992

Getty, I.A.L., and J.W. Warner. *The Kootenay Plains and the Bighorn Wesley Stoney Band: An Oral and Documentary Historical Study, 1800-1970*. Morley, AB: Stoney Tribal Administration Band Council 1972

Hawkes, D. 'Introduction.' In D. Hawkes, ed., *Aboriginal Peoples and Government Responsibility: Exploring Federal and Provincial Roles*. Ottawa: Carleton University Press 1991

Hertzberg, H.W. *The Search for an American Indian Identity*. Syracuse, NY: Syracuse University Press 1971

Kellock, B.W., and F.C.M. Anderson. 'A Theory of Aboriginal Rights.' In F. Cassidy, ed., *Aboriginal Title in British Columbia: Delgamuukw v. The Queen*. Montreal: Institute for Research on Public Policy 1992

Knapp, G. *Native Timber Harvests in Southeast Alaska*. Portland, OR: United States Department of Agriculture, Pacific Northwest Research Station 1992

Madill, D. *British Columbia Indian Treaties in Historical Perspective*. Ottawa: Research Branch, Indian and Northern Affairs Canada, 1981

Mair, C. *Through the Mackenzie Basin: A Narrative of the Athabasca and Peace River Expedition of 1899*. Toronto: University of Toronto Press 1908

Palmer, G. *New Zealand's Constitution in Crisis: Reforming Our Political System*. Dunedin: John McIndoe 1992

Pethick, D. *James Douglas: Servant of Two Empires*. Vancouver: Mitchell Press 1969

Puri, K. 'Copyright Protection for Australian Aborigines in the Light of Mabo.' In M.A. Stephenson and S. Ratnapala, eds., *Mabo: A Judicial Revolution*. St. Lucia, Queensland: University of Queensland Press 1993

Ryder, B. 'The Demise and Rise of the Classical Paradigm in Canadian Federalism: Promoting the Autonomy of the Provinces and First Nations.' *McGill Law Journal* 36 (1991): 308

Slattery, B., 'The Hidden Constitution: Aboriginal Rights in Canada.' In M. Boldt and J.A. Long, eds., *The Quest for Justice: Aboriginal People and Aboriginal Rights*. Toronto: University of Toronto Press 1985

Smith, M. *Our Home or Native Land? What Governments' Aboriginal Policy Is Doing to Canada*. Victoria: Crown Western 1995

Taylor, J.P., and G. Paget. 'Federal/Provincial Responsibility and the Sechelt.' In D. Hawkes, ed., *Aboriginal Peoples and Government Responsibility: Exploring Federal and Provincial Roles*. Ottawa: Carleton University Press 1991

Temm, P. *The Waitangi Tribunal: The Conscience of the Nation*. Auckland: Random Century New Zealand 1990

Tennant, P. *Aboriginal Peoples and Politics: The Indian Land Question in British Columbia, 1849-1989*. Vancouver: UBC Press 1990

Twain, M. *Following the Equator: A Journey Around the World*, vol. 1. Hopewell, NJ: Ecco Press 1992

Whittington, M.S. 'Aboriginal Self-Government in Canada.' In M.S. Whittington and G. Williams, eds., *Canadian Politics in the 1990s*. Toronto: Nelson Canada 1995

Official Documents

Accord of Recognition and Respect [between British Columbia and Gitxsan and Wet'suwet'en]. Hagwilget, BC, 13 June 1994

Agreement Between The First Nations Summit and Her Majesty the Queen in Right of Canada and Her Majesty the Queen in Right of the Province of British Columbia, 21 September 1992

BC Chamber of Commerce. *Policy on Aboriginal Issues*, no date

British Columbia. *British Columbia's Approach to Interim Measures Regarding Lands and Resources*, 30 May 1995

–. *British Columbia's Approach to Treaty Settlements, Lands, and Resources*, 12 May 1995

–. *Papers Connected with the Indian Land Question, 1859-1875*. Victoria: Queen's Printer 1875

Canada. Federal Treaty Negotiations Office (Vancouver). *British Columbia Treaty Negotiations: The Federal Perspective* (Draft), 27 June 1995

–. Department of Indian Affairs and Northern Development. *Indian Register Population by Sex and Residence: 1993*, March 1994

–. Department of Indian and Northern Affairs. Communiqué, 30 September 1994

–. Public Archives of Canada. H.A. Conroy to Superintendent of Indian Affairs (letter),

29 October 1910. RG 10, Black Series, volume 1, file 1/1-11-5-11

–. Public Archives of Canada. J. Douglas to A. Barclay (letter), 3 September 1849. A-11/72.

COFI. *Council of Forest Industries Response to British Columbia's Discussion Papers*, August 1995

Indian Claims Commission. *Submission Guide*. Ottawa: Minister of Supply and Services 1995

KPMG. *Benefits and Costs of Treaty Settlements in British Columbia: A Financial and Economic Perspective*. Project Report, 17 January 1996

Memorandum of Understanding Between Canada and British Columbia Respecting the Sharing of Pre-Treaty Costs, Settlement Costs, Implementation Costs, and the Costs of Self-Government, 21 June 1993

Memorandum of Understanding Respecting the Establishment of a Government-to-Government Relationship Between the Union of B.C. Indian Chiefs and the Government of British Columbia, 11 June 1993

Nisga'a Treaty Negotiations Agreement in Principle, 15 February 1996

Nuu'Chah'Nulth Ha'Wiih Position on Lands, Waters, Air, and Natural Resources, no date

Protocol Between the Province of British Columbia and the Union of BC Municipalities for Implementing the Memorandum of Understanding on Local Government Participation in Aboriginal Treaty Negotiations, 22 March 1993

Protocol Respecting The Government-to-Government Relationship Between the First Nations Summit and the Government of British Columbia, 20 August 1993

Records of Decisions and Commitments by Sechelt, Canada, and British Columbia, 15 July 1995

Report of the British Columbia Claims Task Force, 28 June 1991

Royal Commission on Aboriginal Peoples. *Treaty Making in the Spirit of Co-existence*. Ottawa: Minister of Supply and Services 1995

Sechelt Indian Band. *Sechelt Land Claim* (position paper), February 1995

News Media Articles and Unpublished Papers

'The Alleged Indian Outrage at Jervis Inlet.' *Mainland Guardian*, 24 December 1874

British Columbia. 'Instructions on Open Negotiations,' 19 September 1994

–. News Release, 19 September 1993

'B.C. Native Bands Take to the Barricades to Push Their Cause.' *Maclean's*, 7 August 1995, 10

Dodson, R. 'First Nation Negotiations Better Than Courts and Confrontation.' *Vancouver Sun*, 20 July 1995, B3

Hume, J. 'Hush-Hush Land Claim Costs May Spook the Taxpayers.' *Times-Colonist*, 21 January 1995, A5

'Indian Reservations: How to Succeed, How to Fail.' *The Economist*, 6-12 April 1996, 25-31

'Land Claims Study Released.' *Native Issues Monthly*, February 1996, 13

Palmer, V. ' "Land Claims Process Chaos," Says Forestry Industry.' *Vancouver Sun*, 31 March 1995, A18

–. 'Nisga'a Talks Indicate Land Claims to Cost Billions.' *Vancouver Sun*, 14 July 1995, A18

–. 'Third Parties Blast Land-Claims Secrecy.' *Vancouver Sun*, 30 September 1994

–. 'Third Party in Aboriginal Talks Finds It's Not Invited.' *Vancouver Sun*, 27 March 1995, A10

Pape, A. 'Interim Measures in the B.C. Context.' Paper presented at the Interim Measures During Treaty Negotiations Workshop, Pacific Business and Law Institute, Vancouver, BC, 22 April 1994, 6-7

Peyesiw, Kimowanniwi. Letter to the editor. *Globe and Mail*, 15 September 1995, A18

Slattery, B. 'The Land Rights of Indigenous Canadian Peoples.' Ph.D. diss., University of Saskatchewan 1970

–. 'True Self-Government vs. the Canadian Government's Proposal for Indian Self-Government.' *Kahtou*, 15 May 1994.

Cases

Amodu Tijani v. *Secretary, Southern Nigeria* (1921), 2 Appeal Court, 409

Bear Island Foundation v. *Attorney General of Ontario* (1991), 83 *Dominion Law Reports* (4th), 381

Calder v. *Attorney General of British Columbia* (1973), 34 *Dominion Law Reports* (3d), 328

Calder v. *Attorney General of British Columbia* [1973], *Supreme Court Reports*, 313

Delgamuukw v. *Attorney General of British Columbia* [1991], 5 *Canadian Native Law Reporter*, 1

Delgamuukw v. *The Queen* (1993), 104 *Dominion Law Reports* (4th), 537

Delgamuukw v. *The Queen in Right of the Province of British Columbia and the Attorney General of Canada*, Vancouver Registry CA 013770, 25 June 1993 (B.C.C.A.)

Guerin v. *The Queen*, [1984] 2 *Supreme Court Reports*, 335

Mabo v. *Queensland* (1992), 66 *Australian Law Journal Reports*, 408

Martin, et al. v. *The Queen in Right of the Province of British Columbia, et al.*, [1985] 3 *Western Weekly Reports*, 583 (B.C.C.A.)

Mitchell v. *United States*, 34 *United States Reports* 711 (1835)

R. v. *Sioui*, [1990] 3 *Canadian Native Law Reporter*, 127

Index

Set in Stone by Val Speidel

Printed and bound in Canada by Friesens

Copy-editor: Pat Feindel

Proofreader: Emily Meetsma

Indexer: Annette Lorek

Cartographer: Eric Leinberger